THE LEGEND OF KORRA

Created by
BRYAN KONIETZKO
MICHAEL DANTE DiMARTINO

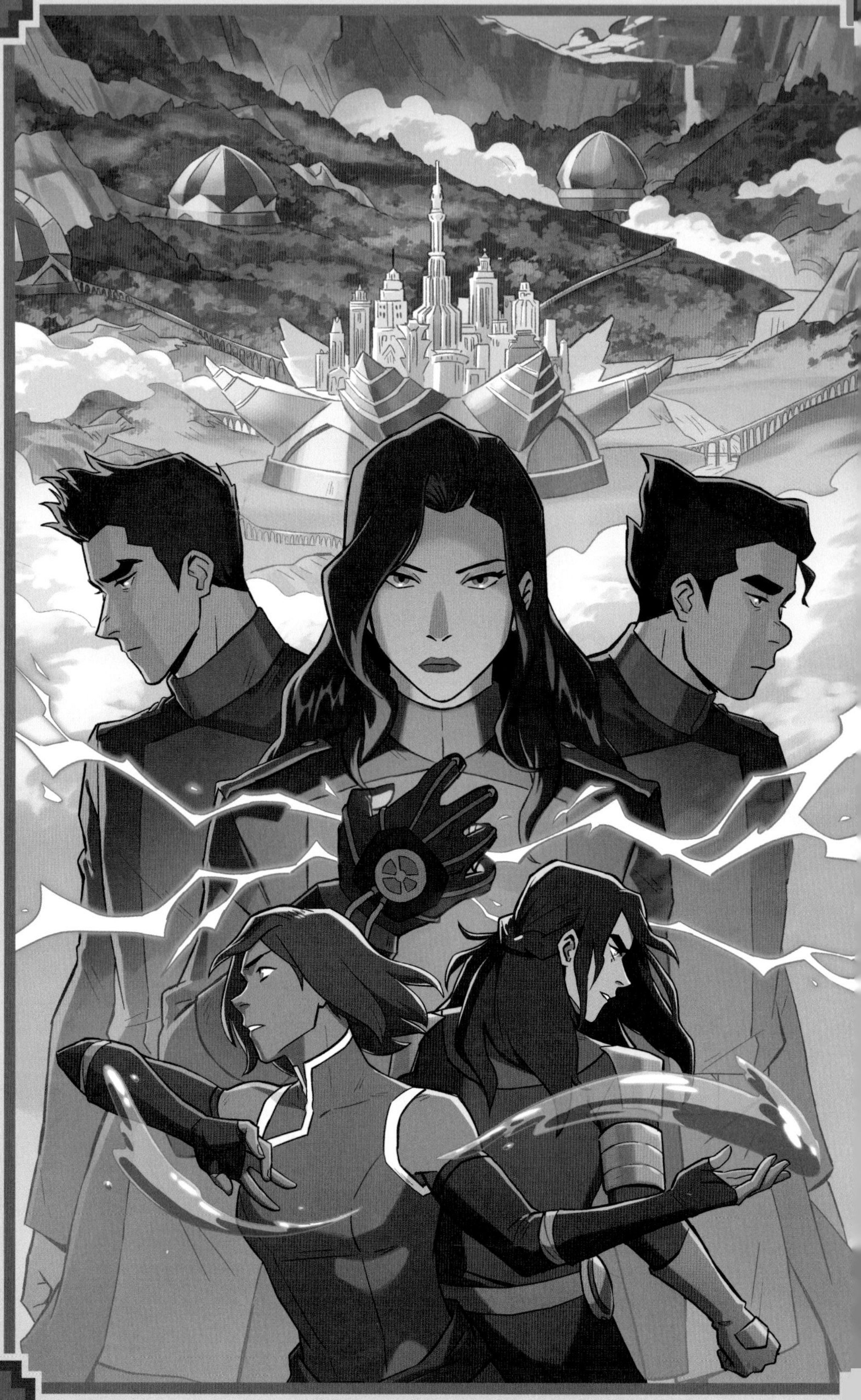

THE LEGEND OF KORRA

RUINS OF THE EMPIRE • PART THREE

written by
MICHAEL DANTE DiMARTINO

art by
MICHELLE WONG

colors by
KILLIAN NG and **ADELE MATERA**

lettering by
ARIANA MAHER

cover by
MICHELLE WONG with **KILLIAN NG**

DARK HORSE BOOKS

president and publisher **MIKE RICHARDSON**

editor **RACHEL ROBERTS**   assistant editor **JENNY BLENK**   designer **SARAH TERRY**

digital art technicians **CHRISTIANNE GILLENARDO-GOUDREAU** and **SAMANTHA HUMMER**

Special thanks to Linda Lee, James Salerno, and Joan Hilty
at Nickelodeon, to Dave Marshall at Dark Horse, and to Bryan
Konietzko, Michael Dante DiMartino, and Tim Hedrick.

Published by **DARK HORSE BOOKS**
A division of Dark Horse Comics LLC
10956 SE Main Street, Milwaukie, OR 97222

DARKHORSE.COM | **NICK.COM**

Comic Shop Locator Service: comicshoplocator.com

First edition: February 2020 | ISBN 978-1-50670-896-6

1 3 5 7 9 10 8 6 4 2
Printed in Canada

Library of Congress Cataloging-in-Publication Data

Names: DiMartino, Michael Dante, writer, creator. | Wong, Michelle (Comic
   book artist), artist. | Ng, Killian, colourist, artist. | Deering,
   Rachel, 1983- letterer.
Title: The legend of Korra : ruins of the empire / written by Michael Dante
   DiMartino ; art by Michelle Wong ; colors by Killian Ng ; lettering by
   Rachel Deering ; cover by Michelle Wong with Killian Ng.
Other titles: Legend of Korra (Television program)
Description: Milwaukie, OR : Dark Horse Books, 2019- | "Created by Bryan
   Konietzko, Michael Dante DiMartino" | Summary: "Korra must decide who to
   trust as the fate of the Earth Kingdom hangs in the balance! On the eve
   of its first elections, the Earth Kingdom finds its future endangered by
   its past. Even as Kuvira stands trial for her crimes, vestiges of her
   imperial ambitions threaten to undermine the nation's democratic hopes.
   But when Korra, Asami, Mako, and Bolin don't all see eye-to-eye as to
   the solution, drastic measures will be taken to halt a new march to
   war!"-- Provided by publisher.
Identifiers: LCCN 2018052018 | ISBN 9781506708942 (part one : paperback) |
   ISBN 9781506708959 (part two : paperback) | ISBN 9781506708966 (part
   three : paperback)
Subjects: LCSH: Comic books, strips, etc. | BISAC: COMICS & GRAPHIC NOVELS
   / Media Tie-In. | COMICS & GRAPHIC NOVELS / Gay & Lesbian.
Classification: LCC PN6728.L434 D54 2019 | DDC 741.5/973--dc23
LC record available at https://lccn.loc.gov/2018052018

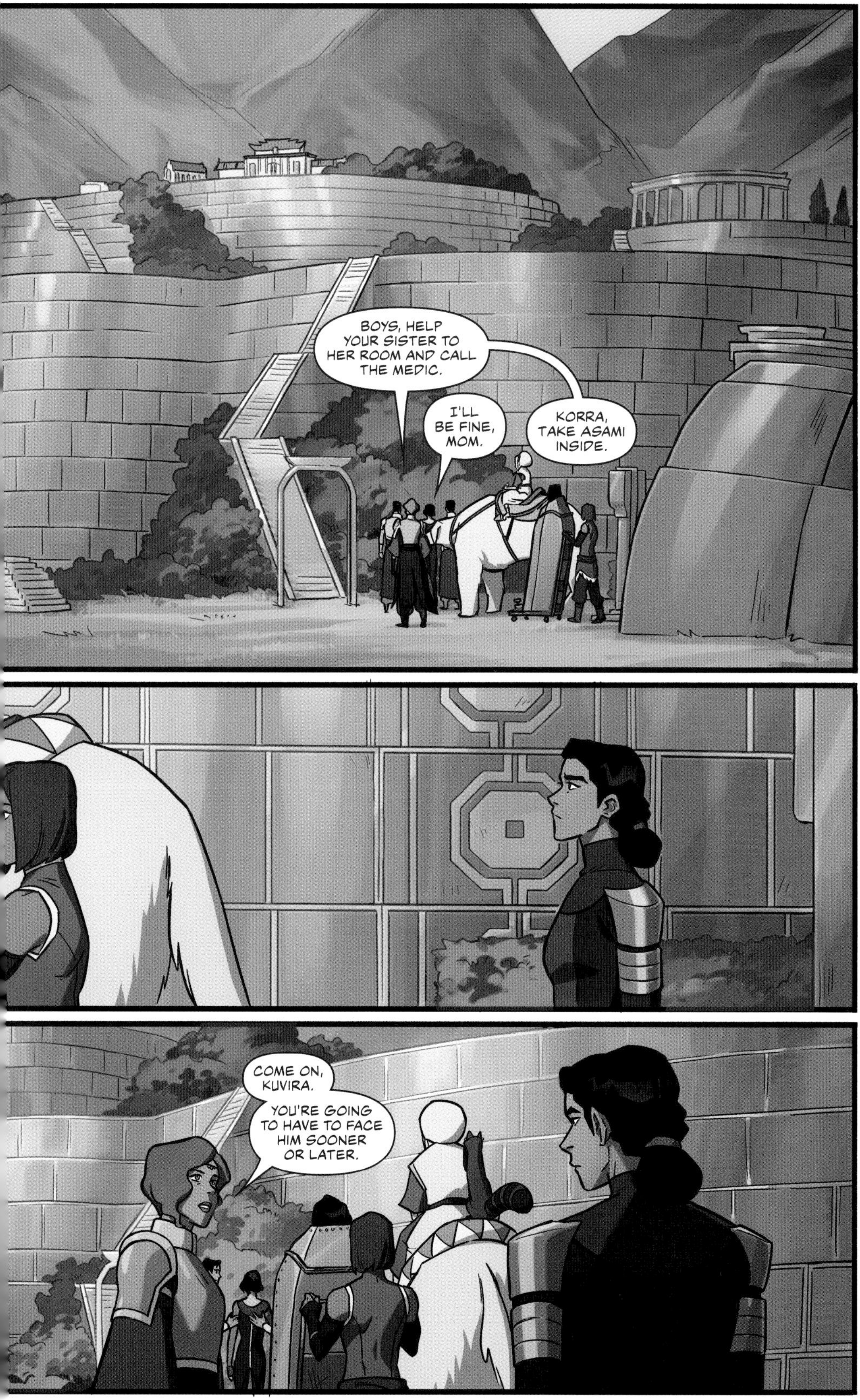
BOYS, HELP YOUR SISTER TO HER ROOM AND CALL THE MEDIC.
KORRA, TAKE ASAMI INSIDE.
I'LL BE FINE, MOM.
COME ON, KUVIRA.
YOU'RE GOING TO HAVE TO FACE HIM SOONER OR LATER.

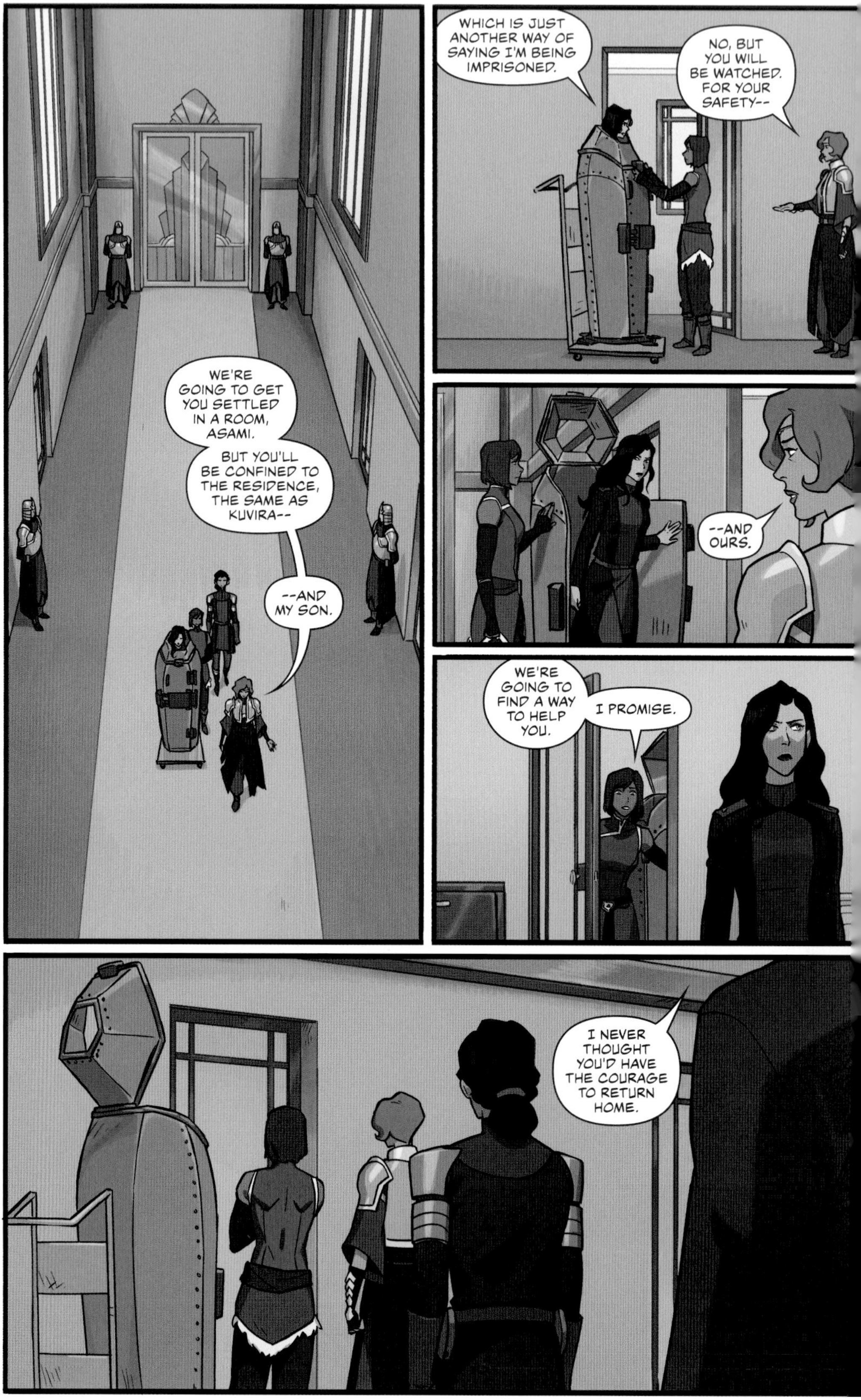

WE'RE GOING TO GET YOU SETTLED IN A ROOM, ASAMI.
BUT YOU'LL BE CONFINED TO THE RESIDENCE, THE SAME AS KUVIRA--
--AND MY SON.
WHICH IS JUST ANOTHER WAY OF SAYING I'M BEING IMPRISONED.
NO, BUT YOU WILL BE WATCHED. FOR YOUR SAFETY--
--AND OURS.
WE'RE GOING TO FIND A WAY TO HELP YOU.
I PROMISE.
I NEVER THOUGHT YOU'D HAVE THE COURAGE TO RETURN HOME.

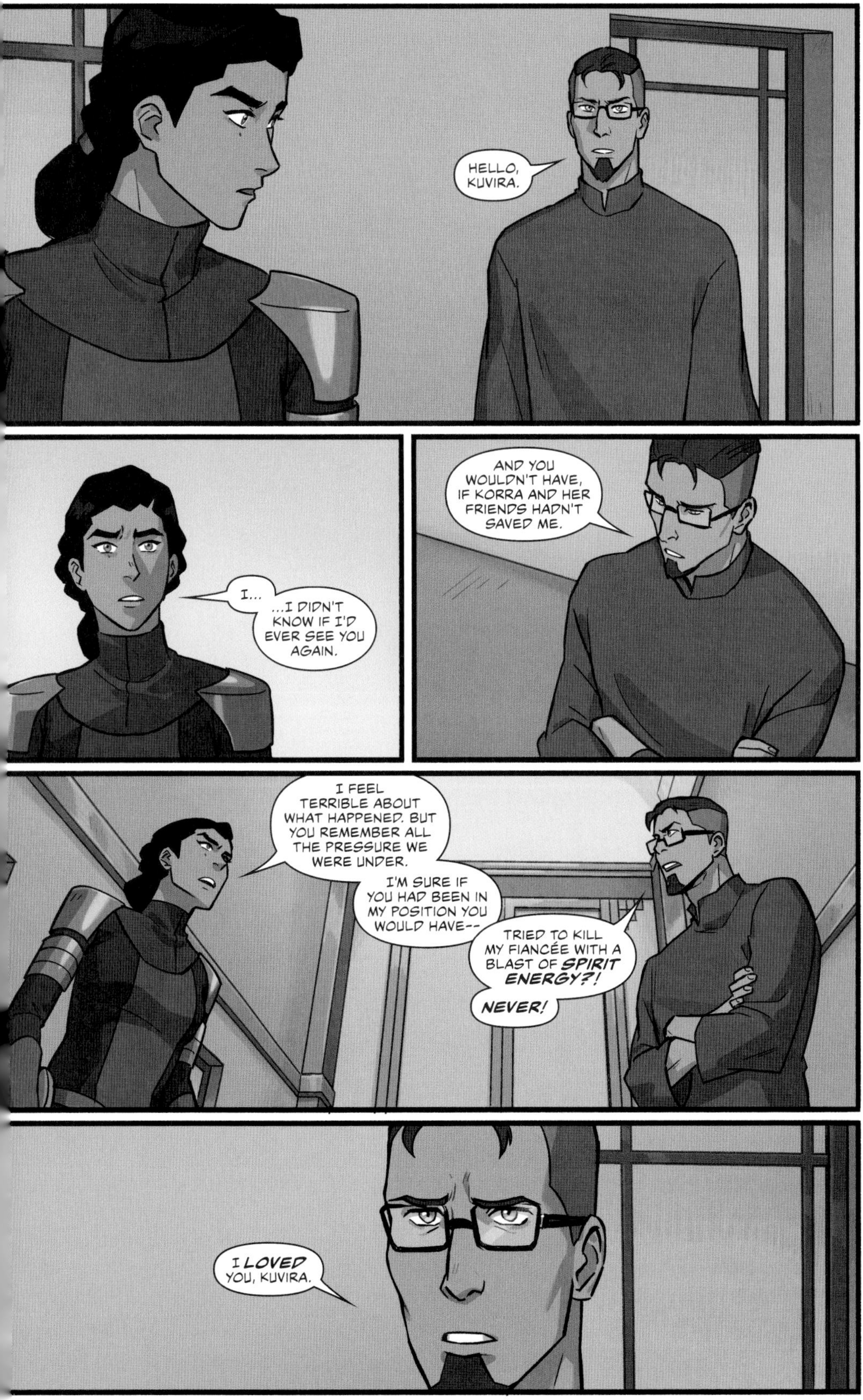
HELLO, KUVIRA.
I... ...I DIDN'T KNOW IF I'D EVER SEE YOU AGAIN.
AND YOU WOULDN'T HAVE, IF KORRA AND HER FRIENDS HADN'T SAVED ME.
I FEEL TERRIBLE ABOUT WHAT HAPPENED. BUT YOU REMEMBER ALL THE PRESSURE WE WERE UNDER.
I'M SURE IF YOU HAD BEEN IN MY POSITION YOU WOULD HAVE--
TRIED TO KILL MY FIANCÉE WITH A BLAST OF *SPIRIT ENERGY?!*
NEVER!
I *LOVED* YOU, KUVIRA.

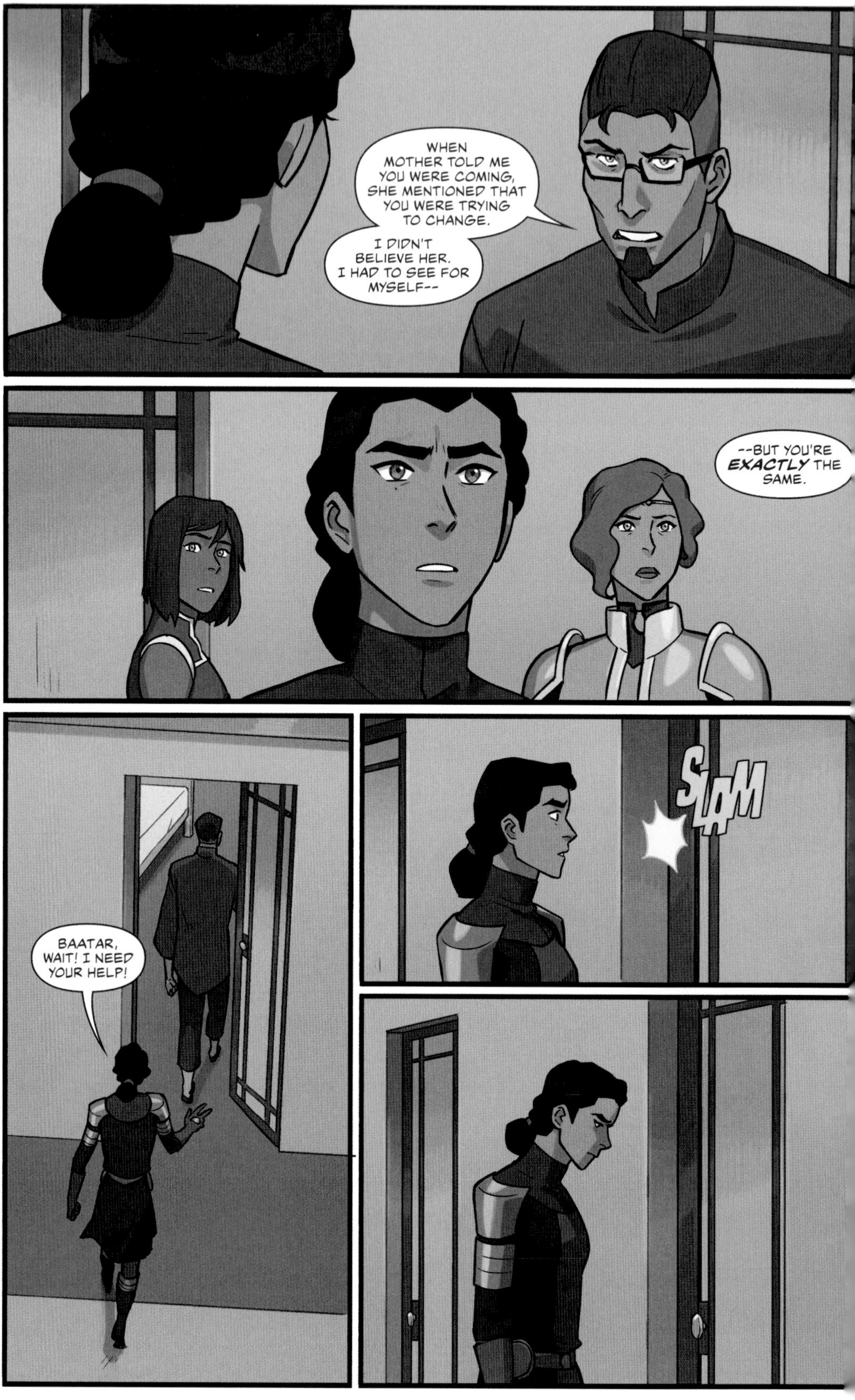

WHEN MOTHER TOLD ME YOU WERE COMING, SHE MENTIONED THAT YOU WERE TRYING TO CHANGE.
I DIDN'T BELIEVE HER. I HAD TO SEE FOR MYSELF--
--BUT YOU'RE *EXACTLY* THE SAME.
BAATAR, WAIT! I NEED YOUR HELP!
SLAM

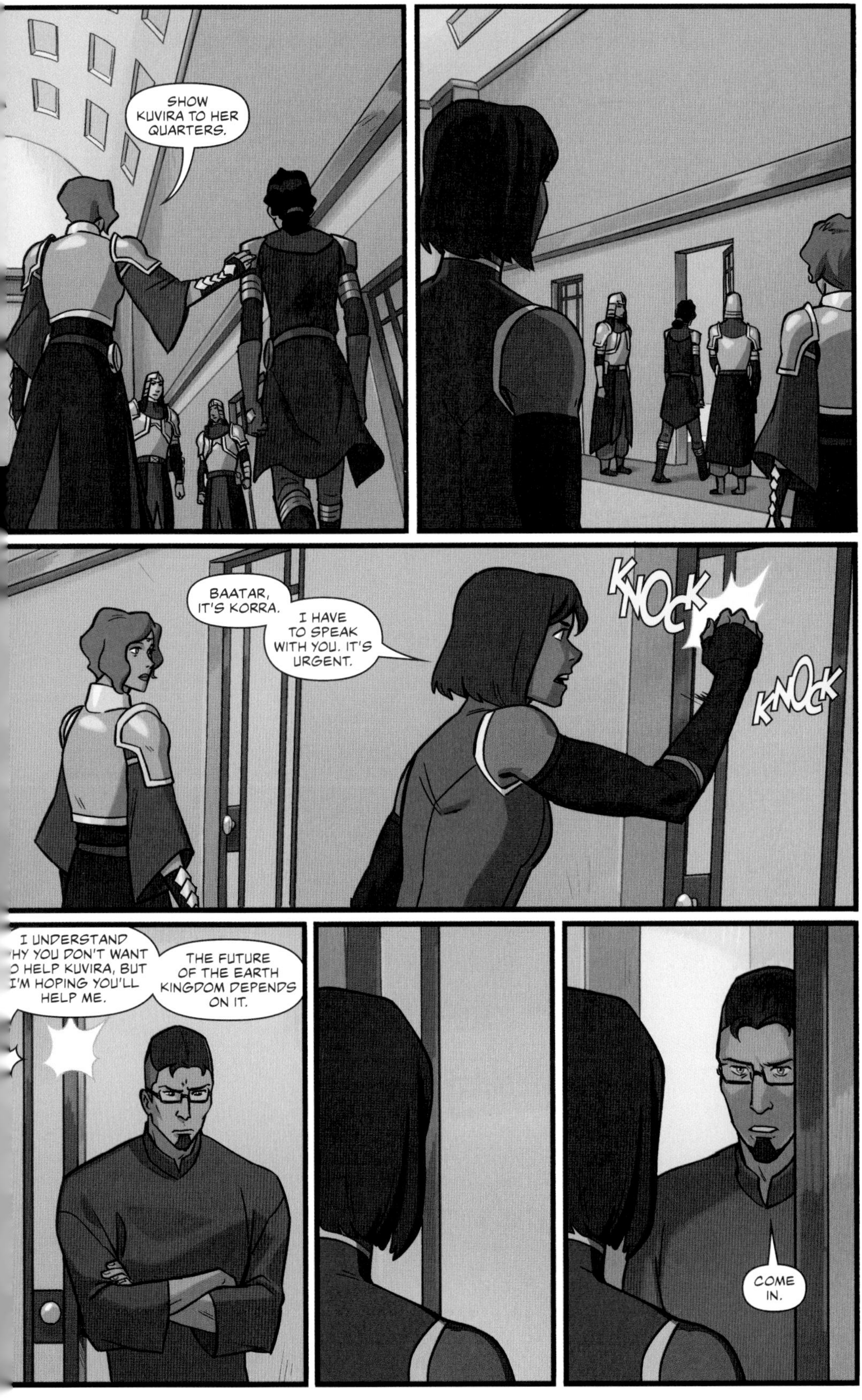

SHOW KUVIRA TO HER QUARTERS.
KNOCK
KNOCK
BAATAR, IT'S KORRA.
I HAVE TO SPEAK WITH YOU. IT'S URGENT.
I UNDERSTAND WHY YOU DON'T WANT TO HELP KUVIRA, BUT I'M HOPING YOU'LL HELP ME.
THE FUTURE OF THE EARTH KINGDOM DEPENDS ON IT.
COME IN.

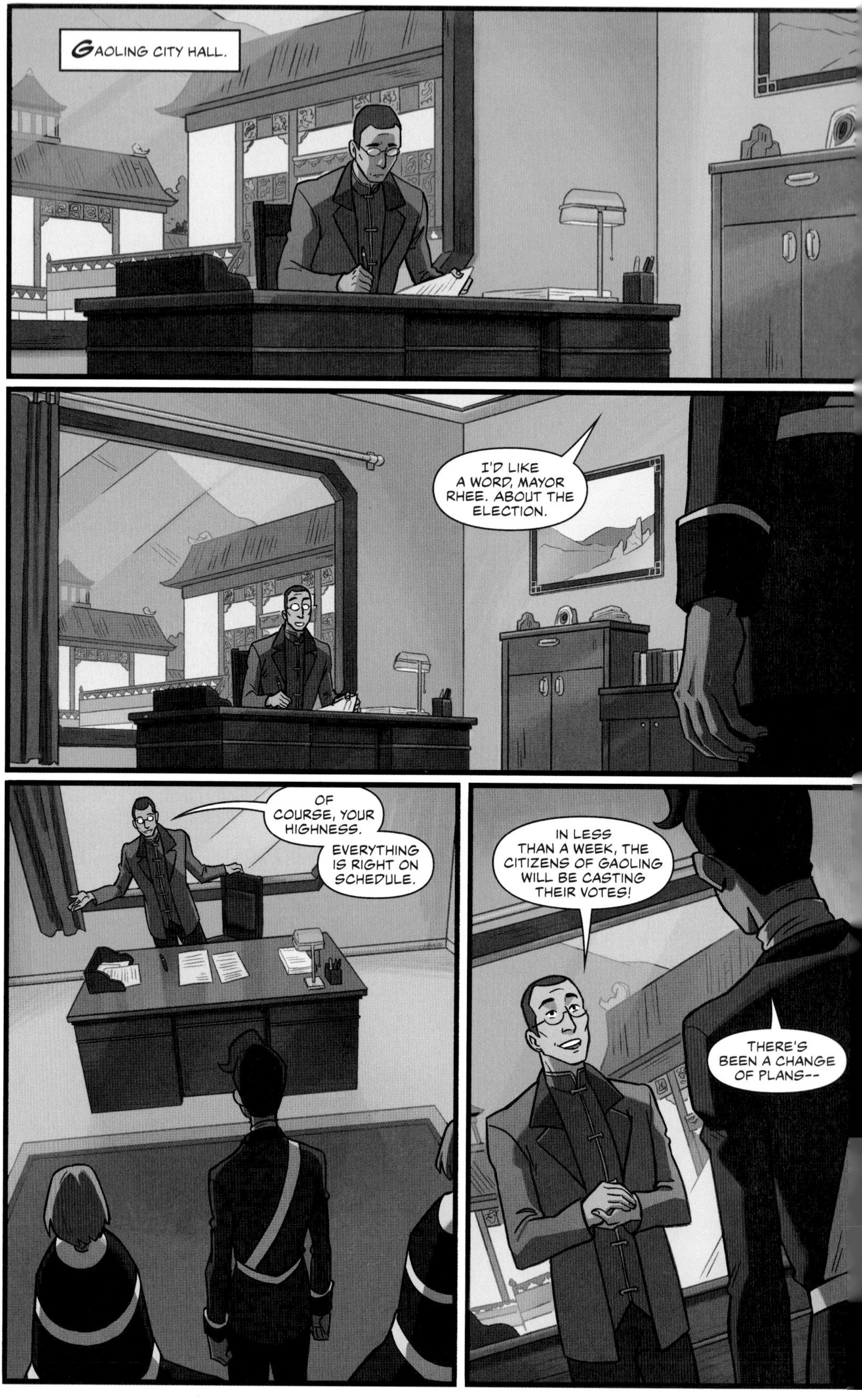

GAOLING CITY HALL.
I'D LIKE A WORD, MAYOR RHEE. ABOUT THE ELECTION.
OF COURSE, YOUR HIGHNESS.
EVERYTHING IS RIGHT ON SCHEDULE.
IN LESS THAN A WEEK, THE CITIZENS OF GAOLING WILL BE CASTING THEIR VOTES!
THERE'S BEEN A CHANGE OF PLANS--

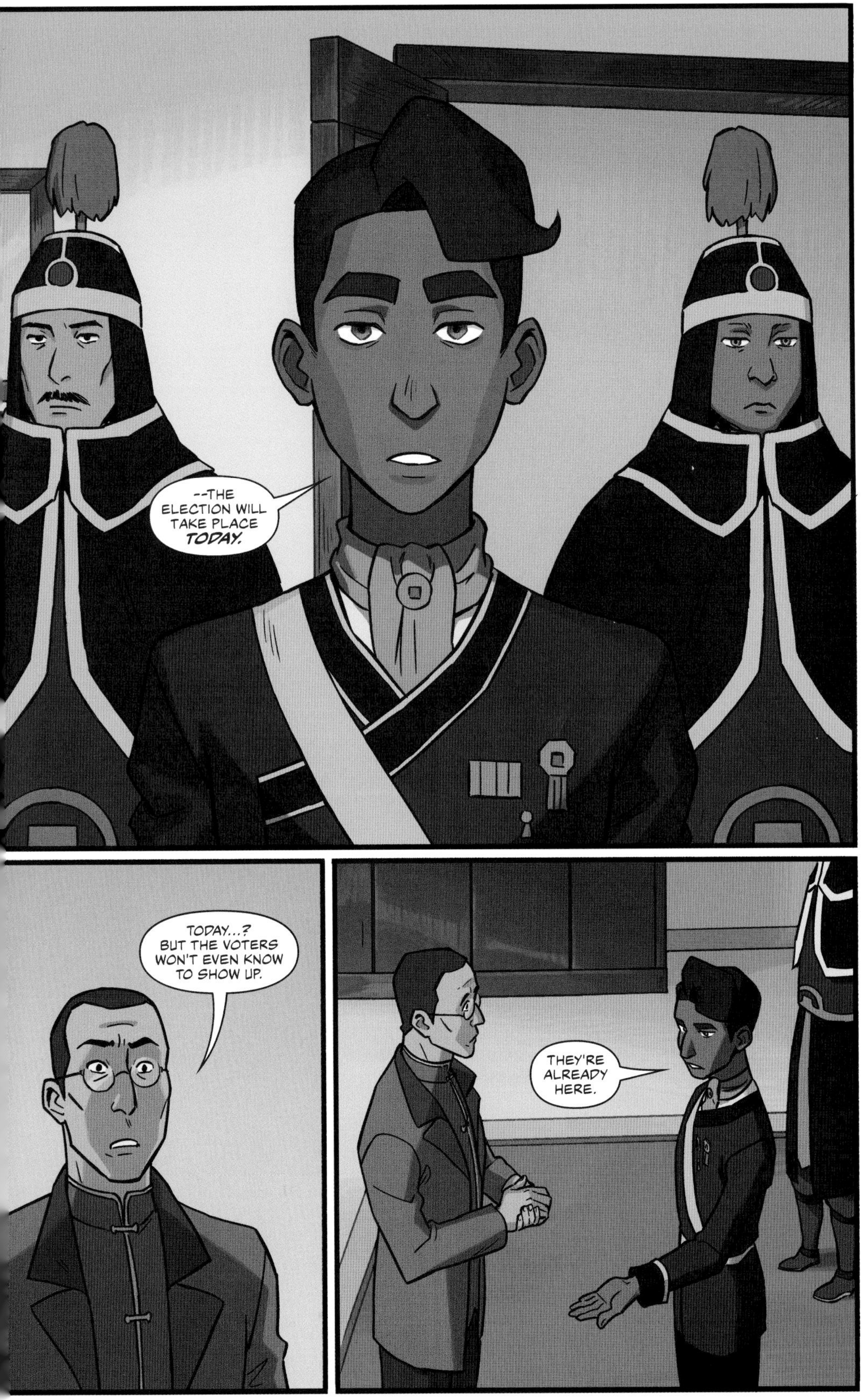
--THE ELECTION WILL TAKE PLACE *TODAY.*
TODAY...? BUT THE VOTERS WON'T EVEN KNOW TO SHOW UP.
THEY'RE ALREADY HERE.

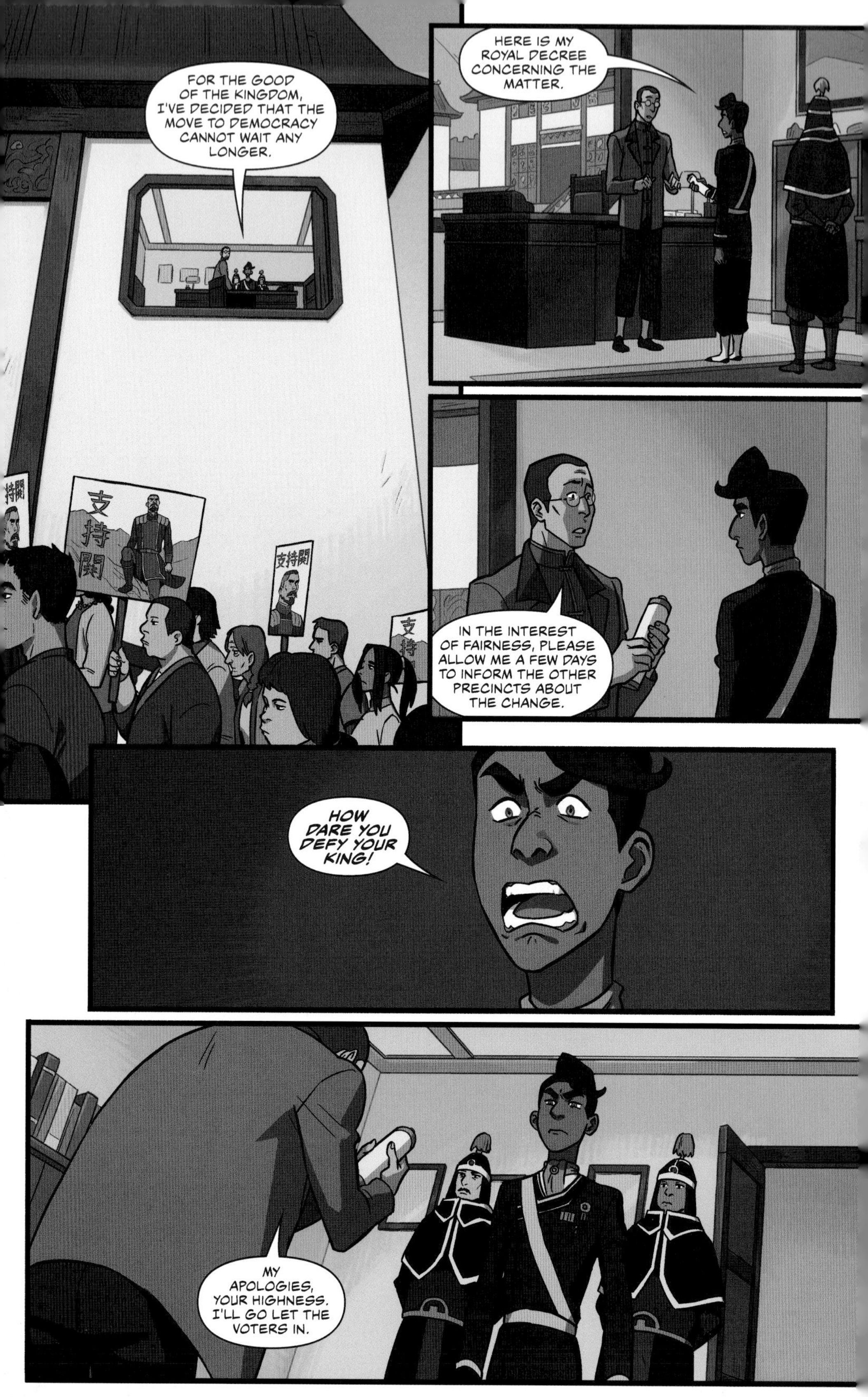
FOR THE GOOD OF THE KINGDOM, I'VE DECIDED THAT THE MOVE TO DEMOCRACY CANNOT WAIT ANY LONGER.
支持関
HERE IS MY ROYAL DECREE CONCERNING THE MATTER.
IN THE INTEREST OF FAIRNESS, PLEASE ALLOW ME A FEW DAYS TO INFORM THE OTHER PRECINCTS ABOUT THE CHANGE.
HOW DARE YOU DEFY YOUR KING!
MY APOLOGIES, YOUR HIGHNESS. I'LL GO LET THE VOTERS IN.

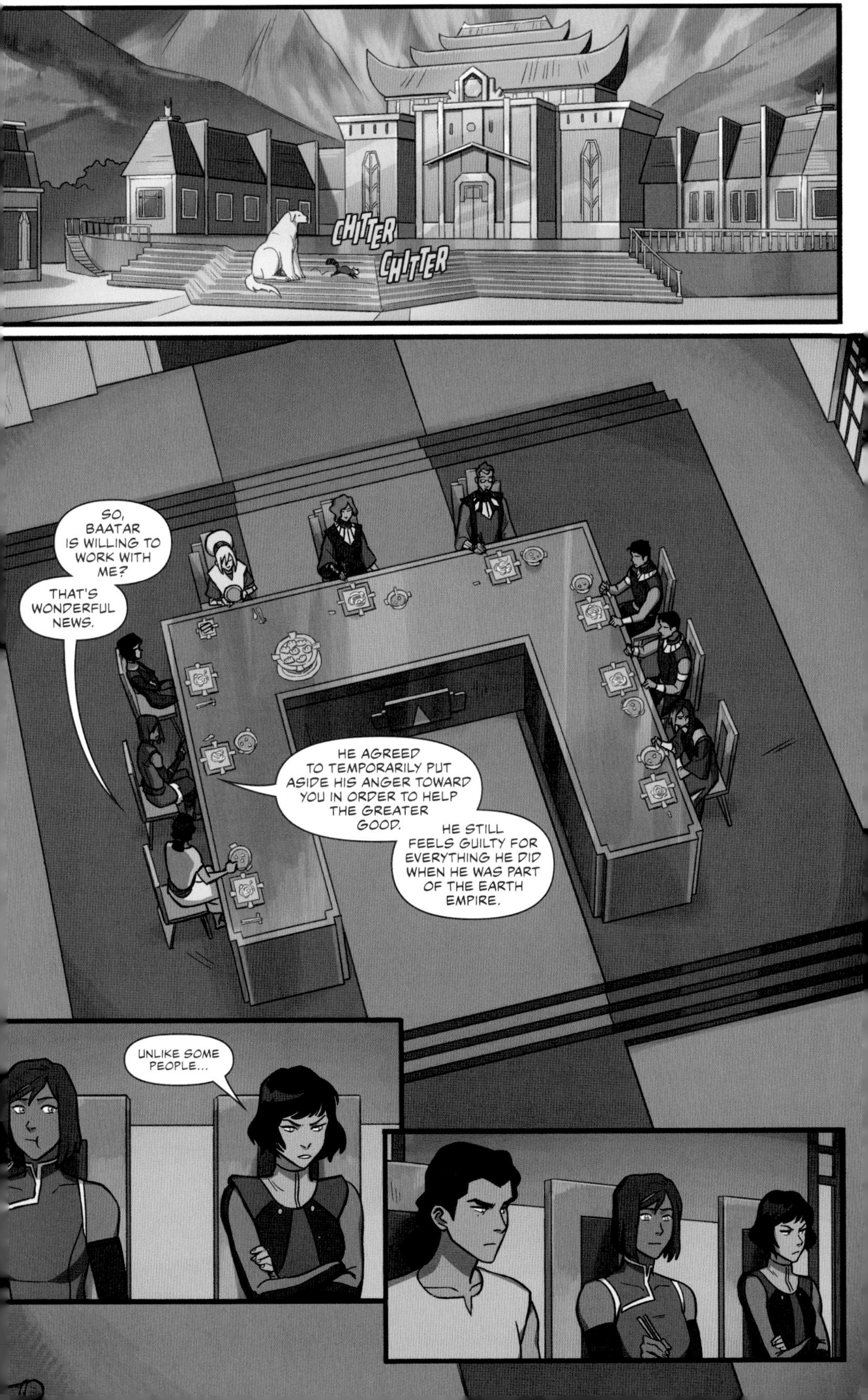
CHITTER
CHITTER
SO, BAATAR IS WILLING TO WORK WITH ME?
THAT'S WONDERFUL NEWS.
HE AGREED TO TEMPORARILY PUT ASIDE HIS ANGER TOWARD YOU IN ORDER TO HELP THE GREATER GOOD.
HE STILL FEELS GUILTY FOR EVERYTHING HE DID WHEN HE WAS PART OF THE EARTH EMPIRE.
UNLIKE SOME PEOPLE...

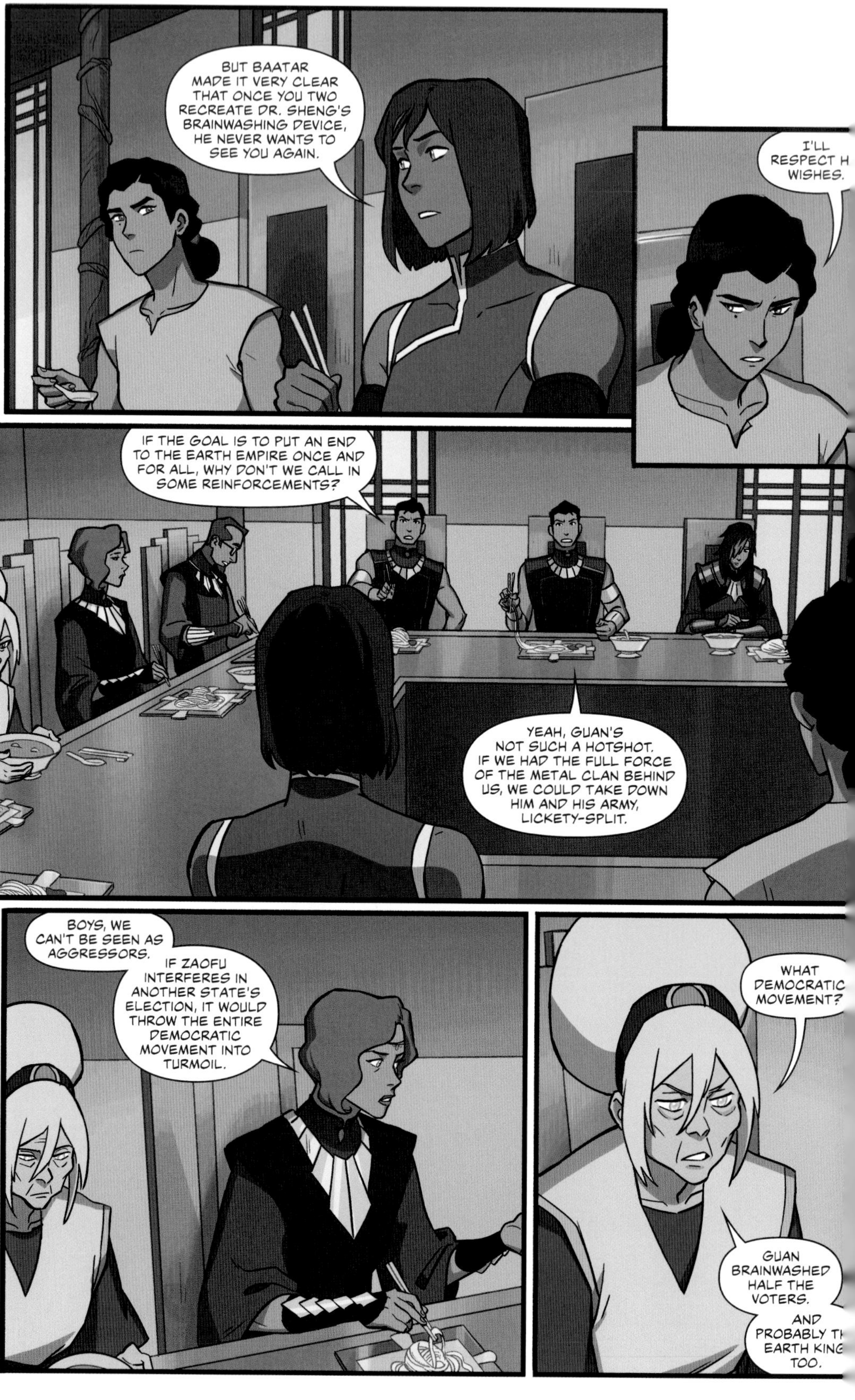
BUT BAATAR MADE IT VERY CLEAR THAT ONCE YOU TWO RECREATE DR. SHENG'S BRAINWASHING DEVICE, HE NEVER WANTS TO SEE YOU AGAIN.
I'LL RESPECT H WISHES.
IF THE GOAL IS TO PUT AN END TO THE EARTH EMPIRE ONCE AND FOR ALL, WHY DON'T WE CALL IN SOME REINFORCEMENTS?
YEAH, GUAN'S NOT SUCH A HOTSHOT. IF WE HAD THE FULL FORCE OF THE METAL CLAN BEHIND US, WE COULD TAKE DOWN HIM AND HIS ARMY, LICKETY-SPLIT.
BOYS, WE CAN'T BE SEEN AS AGGRESSORS.
IF ZAOFU INTERFERES IN ANOTHER STATE'S ELECTION, IT WOULD THROW THE ENTIRE DEMOCRATIC MOVEMENT INTO TURMOIL.
WHAT DEMOCRATIC MOVEMENT?
GUAN BRAINWASHED HALF THE VOTERS.
AND PROBABLY T EARTH KING TOO.

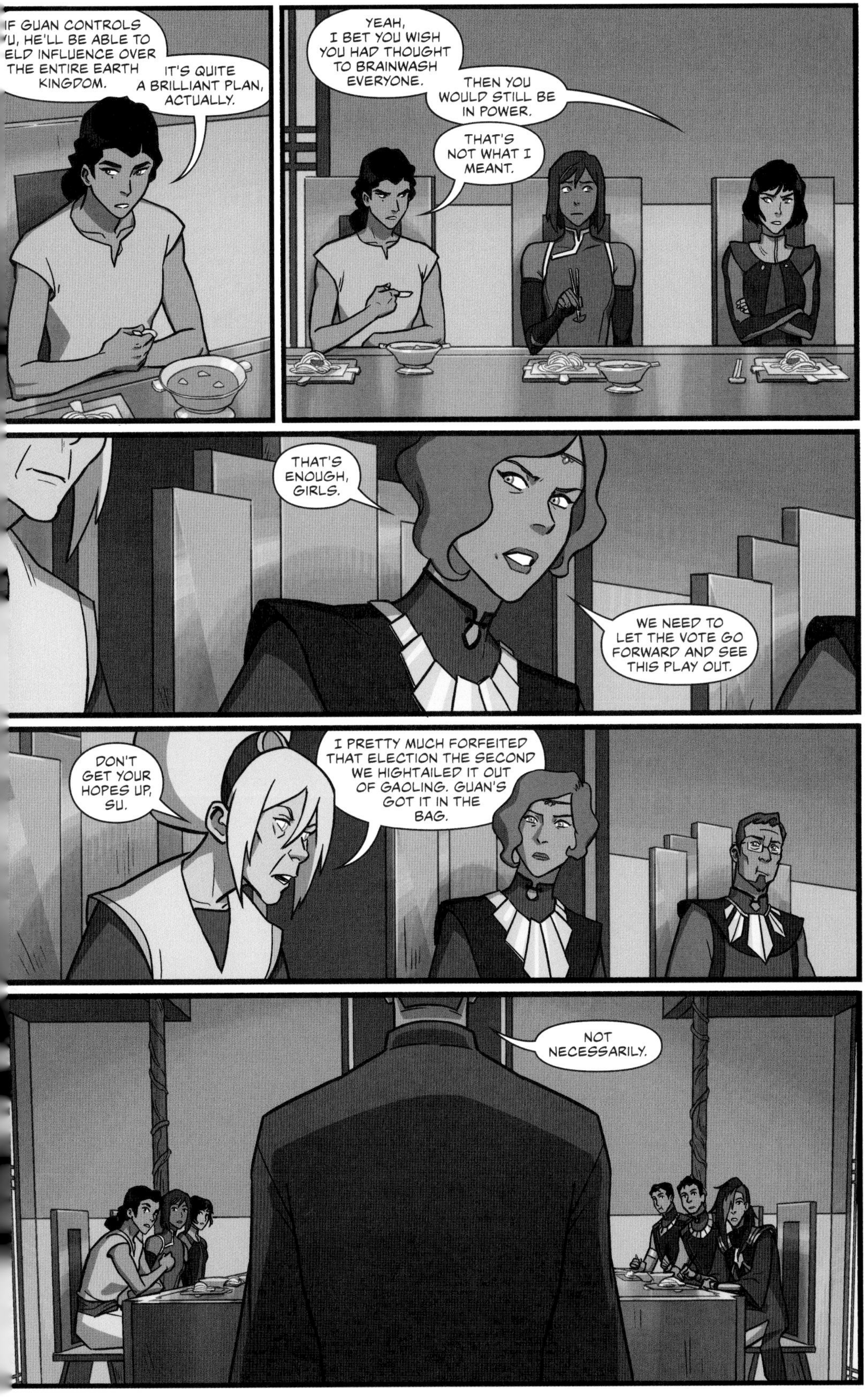
IF GUAN CONTROLS 'U, HE'LL BE ABLE TO ELD INFLUENCE OVER THE ENTIRE EARTH KINGDOM.
IT'S QUITE A BRILLIANT PLAN, ACTUALLY.
YEAH, I BET YOU WISH YOU HAD THOUGHT TO BRAINWASH EVERYONE.
THEN YOU WOULD STILL BE IN POWER.
THAT'S NOT WHAT I MEANT.
THAT'S ENOUGH, GIRLS.
WE NEED TO LET THE VOTE GO FORWARD AND SEE THIS PLAY OUT.
DON'T GET YOUR HOPES UP, SU.
I PRETTY MUCH FORFEITED THAT ELECTION THE SECOND WE HIGHTAILED IT OUT OF GAOLING. GUAN'S GOT IT IN THE BAG.
NOT NECESSARILY.

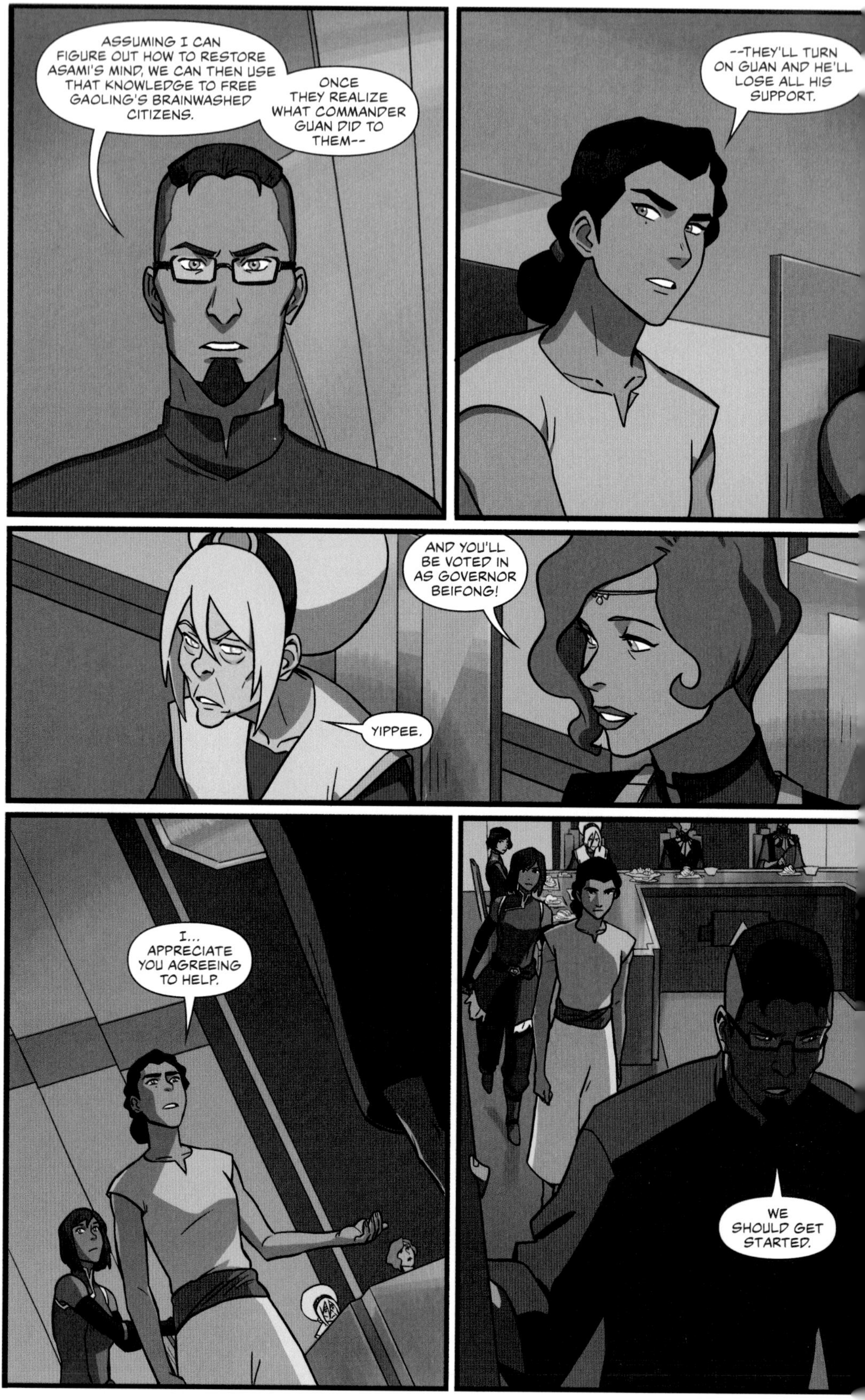
ASSUMING I CAN FIGURE OUT HOW TO RESTORE ASAMI'S MIND, WE CAN THEN USE THAT KNOWLEDGE TO FREE GAOLING'S BRAINWASHED CITIZENS.
ONCE THEY REALIZE WHAT COMMANDER GUAN DID TO THEM--
--THEY'LL TURN ON GUAN AND HE'LL LOSE ALL HIS SUPPORT.
AND YOU'LL BE VOTED IN AS GOVERNOR BEIFONG!
YIPPEE.
I... APPRECIATE YOU AGREEING TO HELP.
WE SHOULD GET STARTED.

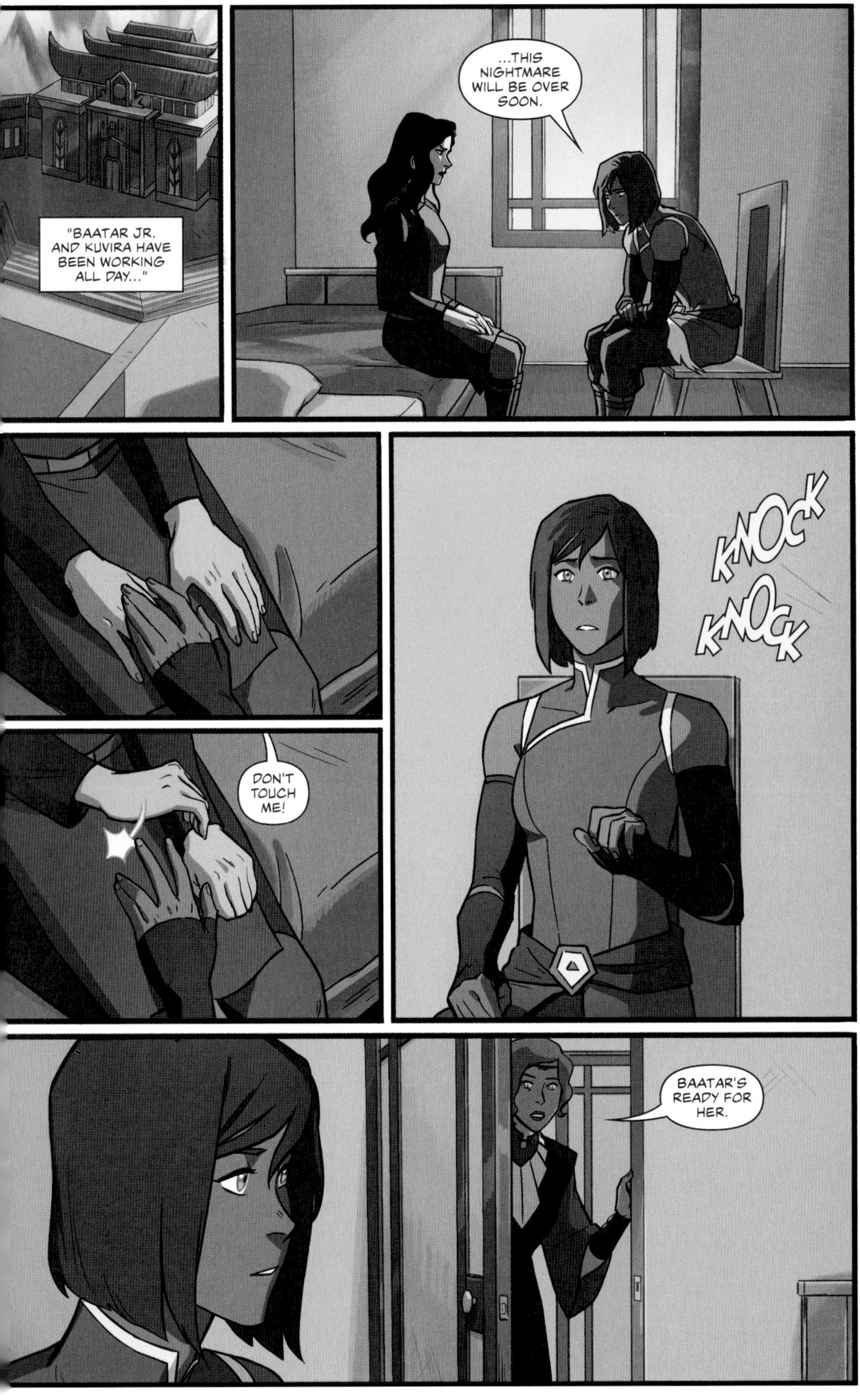
"BAATAR JR. AND KUVIRA HAVE BEEN WORKING ALL DAY..."
...THIS NIGHTMARE WILL BE OVER SOON.
DON'T TOUCH ME!
KNOCK KNOCK
BAATAR'S READY FOR HER.

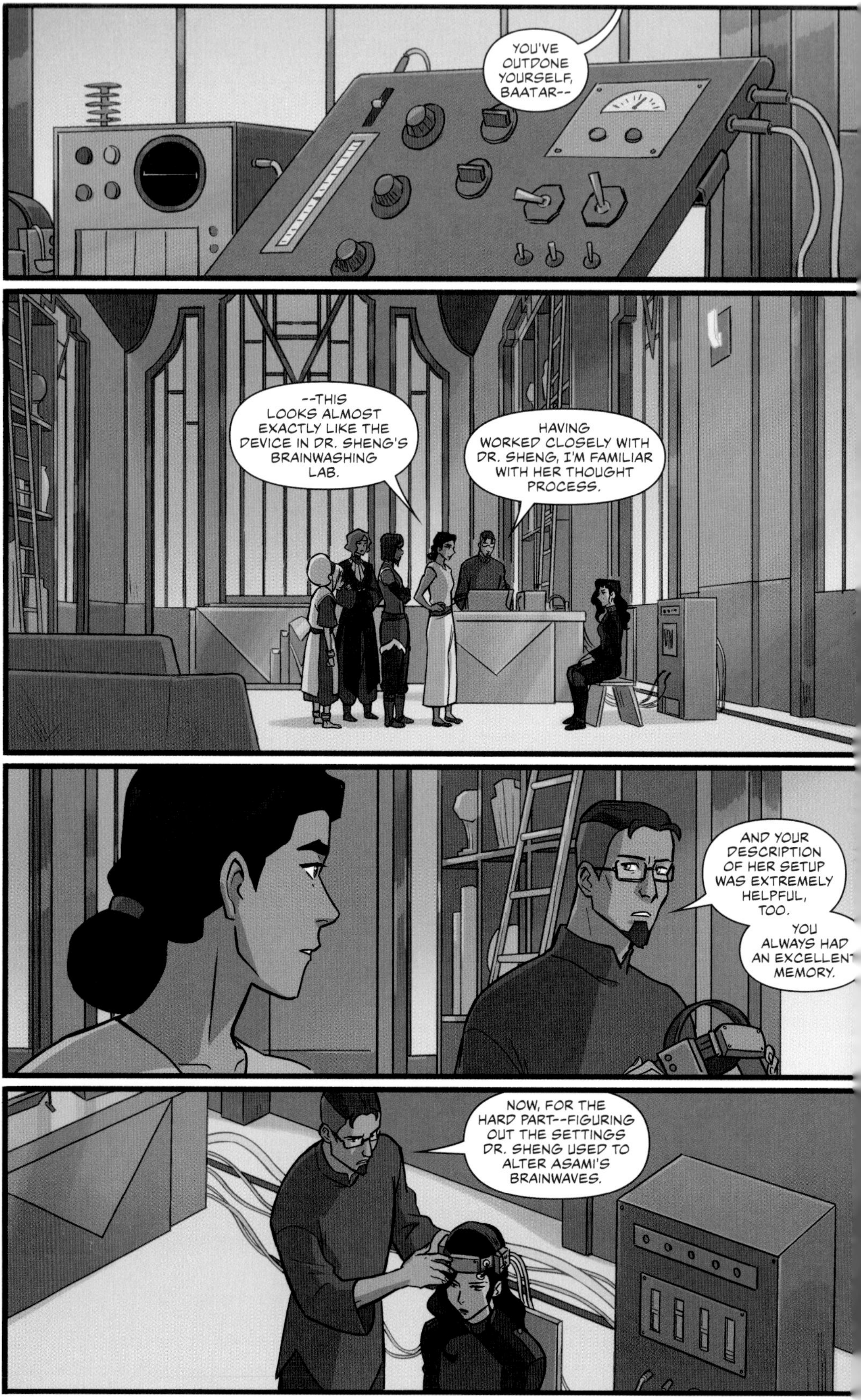
YOU'VE OUTDONE YOURSELF, BAATAR--
--THIS LOOKS ALMOST EXACTLY LIKE THE DEVICE IN DR. SHENG'S BRAINWASHING LAB.
HAVING WORKED CLOSELY WITH DR. SHENG, I'M FAMILIAR WITH HER THOUGHT PROCESS.
AND YOUR DESCRIPTION OF HER SETUP WAS EXTREMELY HELPFUL, TOO.
YOU ALWAYS HAD AN EXCELLENT MEMORY.
NOW, FOR THE HARD PART--FIGURING OUT THE SETTINGS DR. SHENG USED TO ALTER ASAMI'S BRAINWAVES.

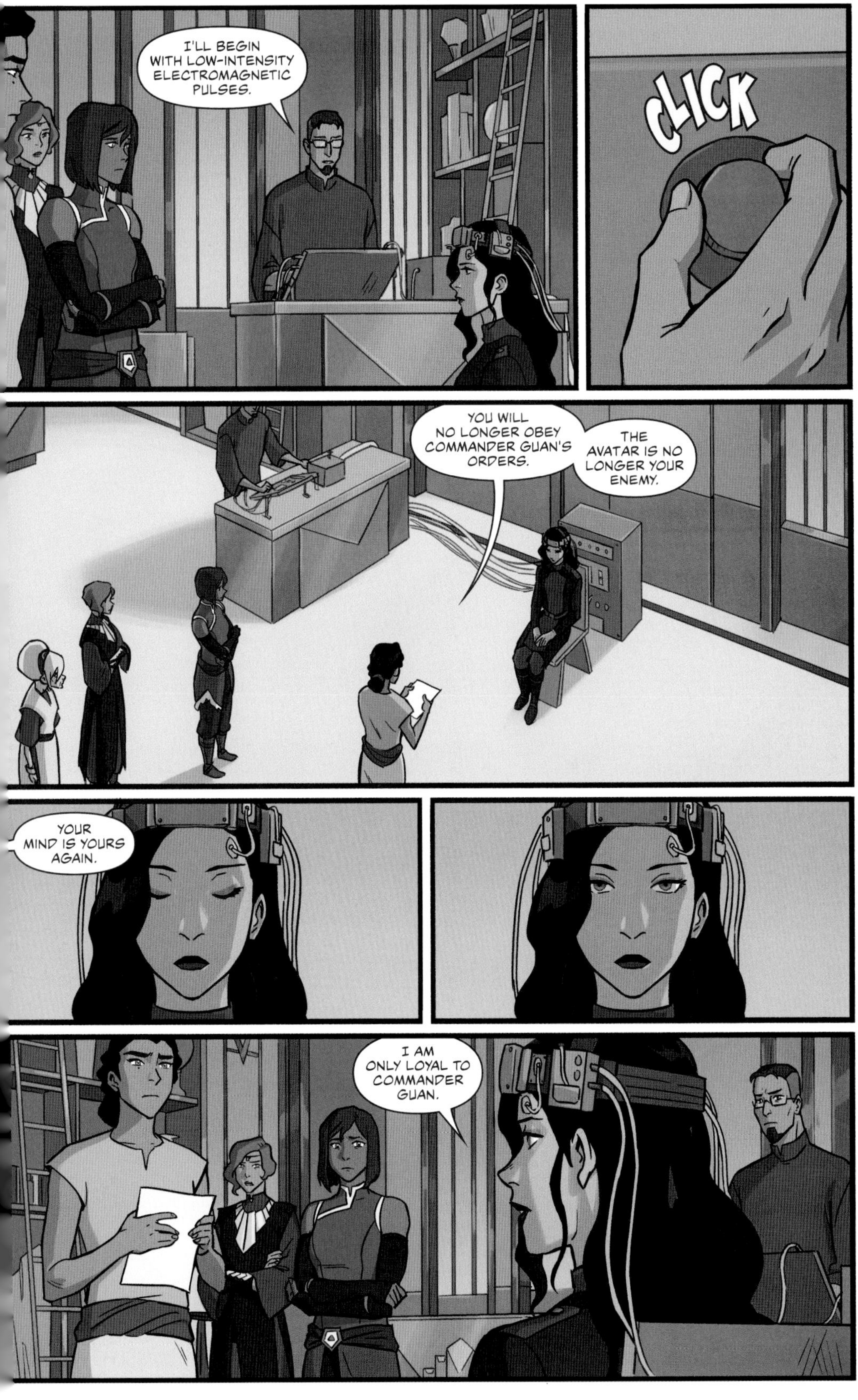
I'LL BEGIN WITH LOW-INTENSITY ELECTROMAGNETIC PULSES.
CLICK
YOU WILL NO LONGER OBEY COMMANDER GUAN'S ORDERS.
THE AVATAR IS NO LONGER YOUR ENEMY.
YOUR MIND IS YOURS AGAIN.
I AM ONLY LOYAL TO COMMANDER GUAN.

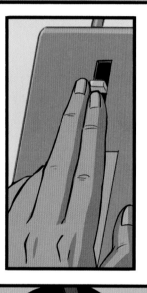

YOU WILL NO LONGER OBEY COMMANDER GUAN'S ORDERS.

THE AVATAR IS NO LONGER YOUR ENEMY.

YOUR MIND IS YOURS AGAIN.

I AM ONLY LOYAL TO COMMANDER GUAN.

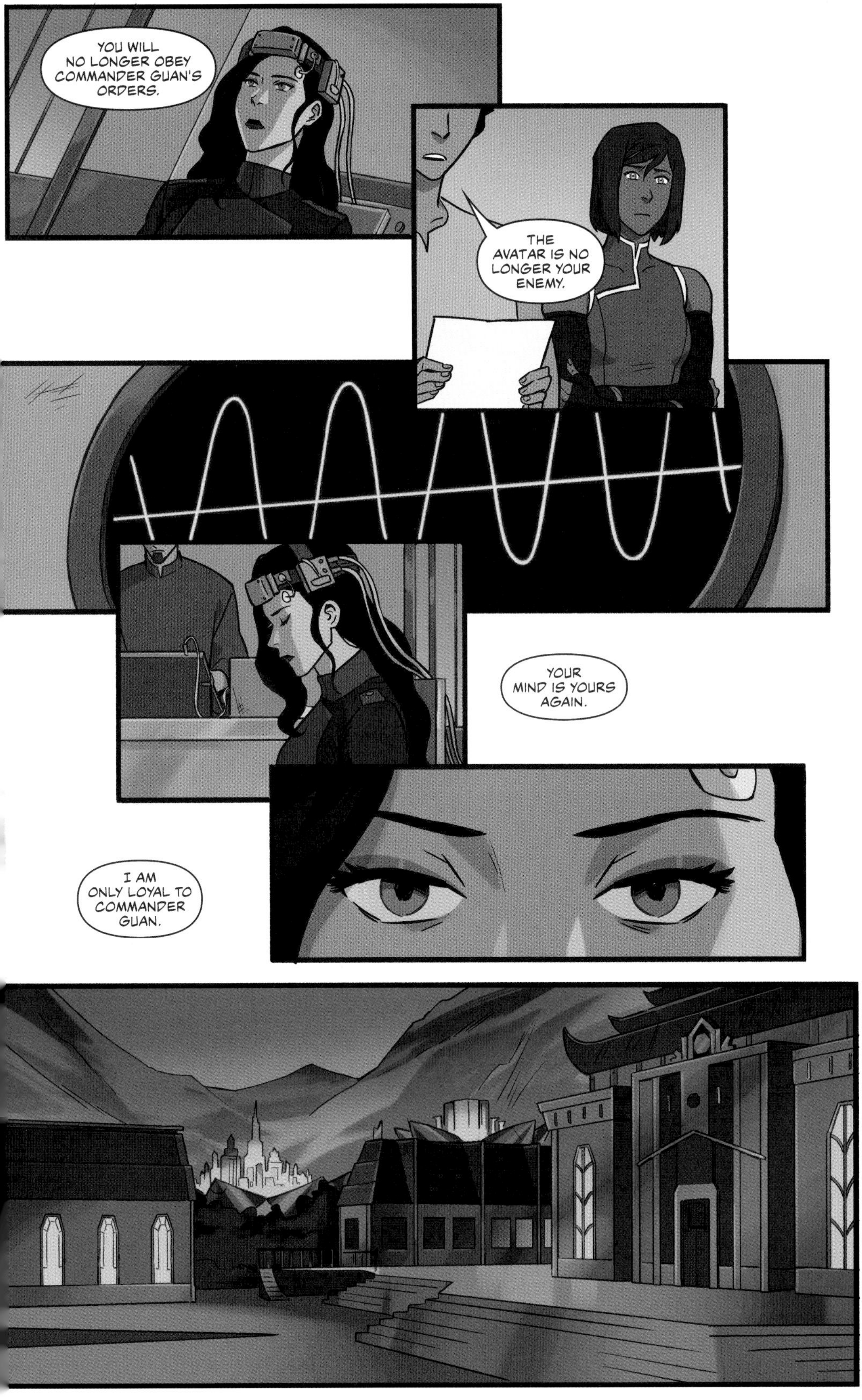
YOU WILL NO LONGER OBEY COMMANDER GUAN'S ORDERS.
THE AVATAR IS NO LONGER YOUR ENEMY.
YOUR MIND IS YOURS AGAIN.
I AM ONLY LOYAL TO COMMANDER GUAN.

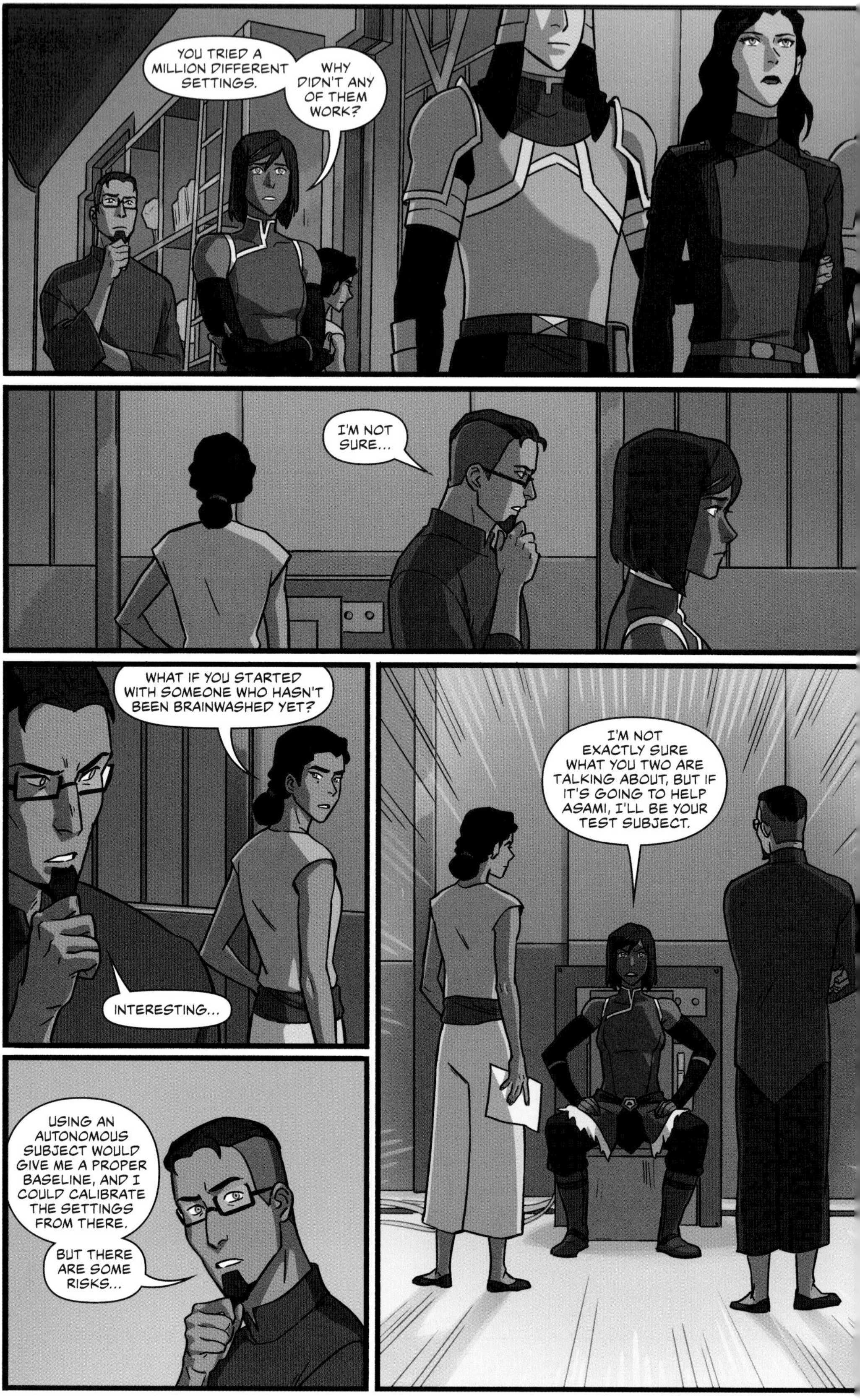
YOU TRIED A MILLION DIFFERENT SETTINGS.
WHY DIDN'T ANY OF THEM WORK?
I'M NOT SURE...
WHAT IF YOU STARTED WITH SOMEONE WHO HASN'T BEEN BRAINWASHED YET?
INTERESTING...
USING AN AUTONOMOUS SUBJECT WOULD GIVE ME A PROPER BASELINE, AND I COULD CALIBRATE THE SETTINGS FROM THERE.
BUT THERE ARE SOME RISKS...
I'M NOT EXACTLY SURE WHAT YOU TWO ARE TALKING ABOUT, BUT IF IT'S GOING TO HELP ASAMI, I'LL BE YOUR TEST SUBJECT.

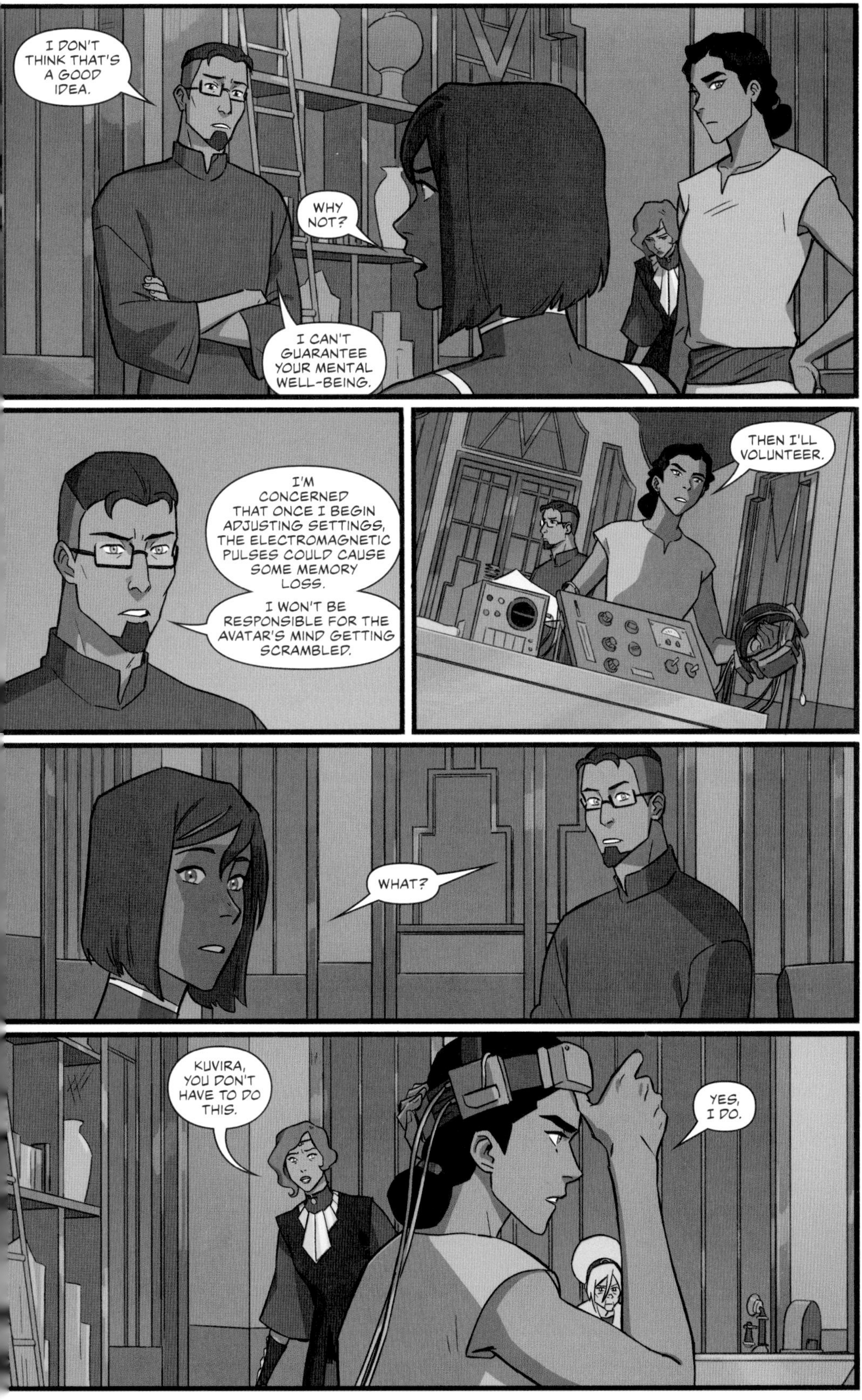
I DON'T THINK THAT'S A GOOD IDEA.
WHY NOT?
I CAN'T GUARANTEE YOUR MENTAL WELL-BEING.
I'M CONCERNED THAT ONCE I BEGIN ADJUSTING SETTINGS, THE ELECTROMAGNETIC PULSES COULD CAUSE SOME MEMORY LOSS.
I WON'T BE RESPONSIBLE FOR THE AVATAR'S MIND GETTING SCRAMBLED.
THEN I'LL VOLUNTEER.
WHAT?
KUVIRA, YOU DON'T HAVE TO DO THIS.
YES, I DO.

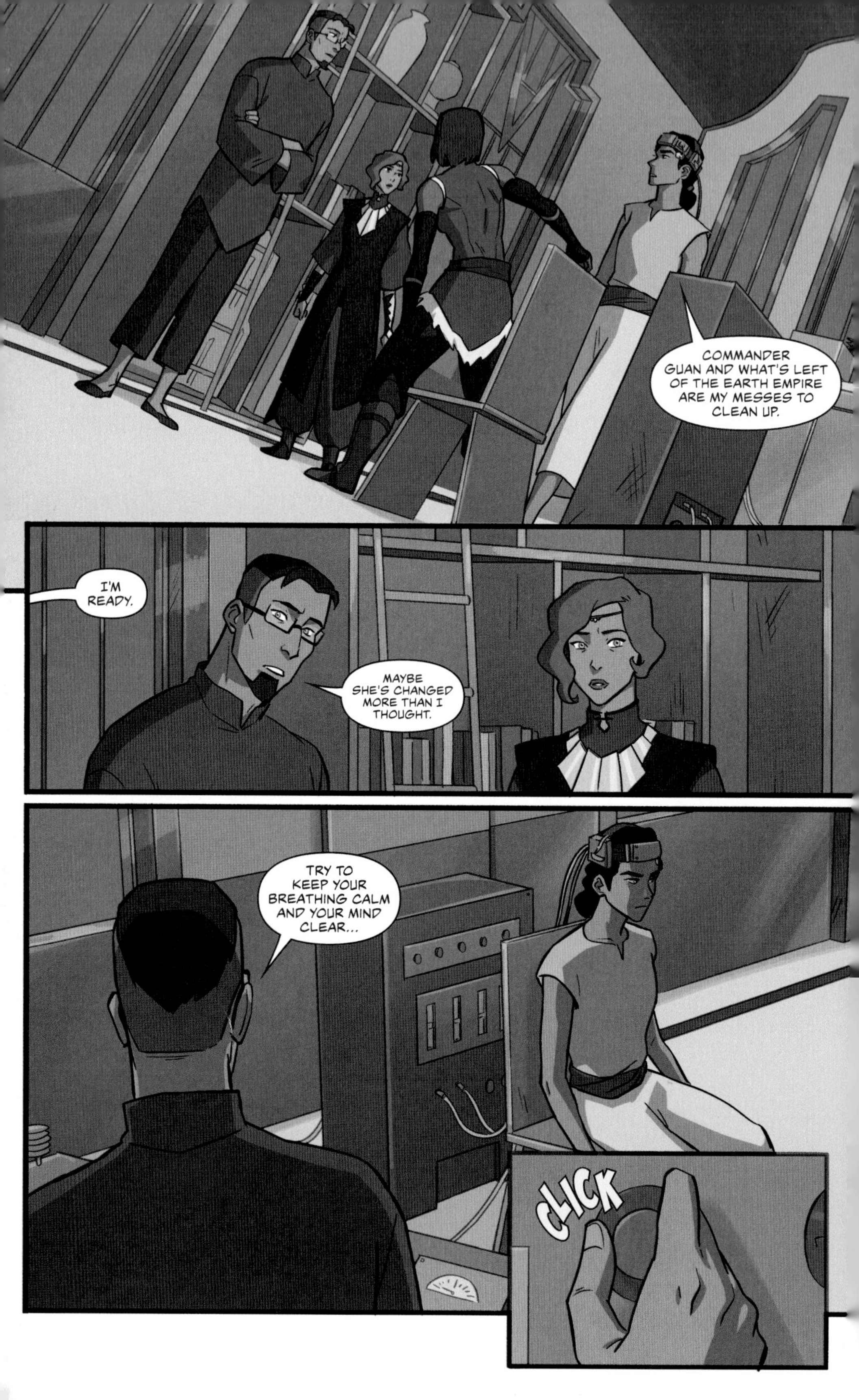
COMMANDER GUAN AND WHAT'S LEFT OF THE EARTH EMPIRE ARE MY MESSES TO CLEAN UP.
I'M READY.
MAYBE SHE'S CHANGED MORE THAN I THOUGHT.
TRY TO KEEP YOUR BREATHING CALM AND YOUR MIND CLEAR...
CLICK

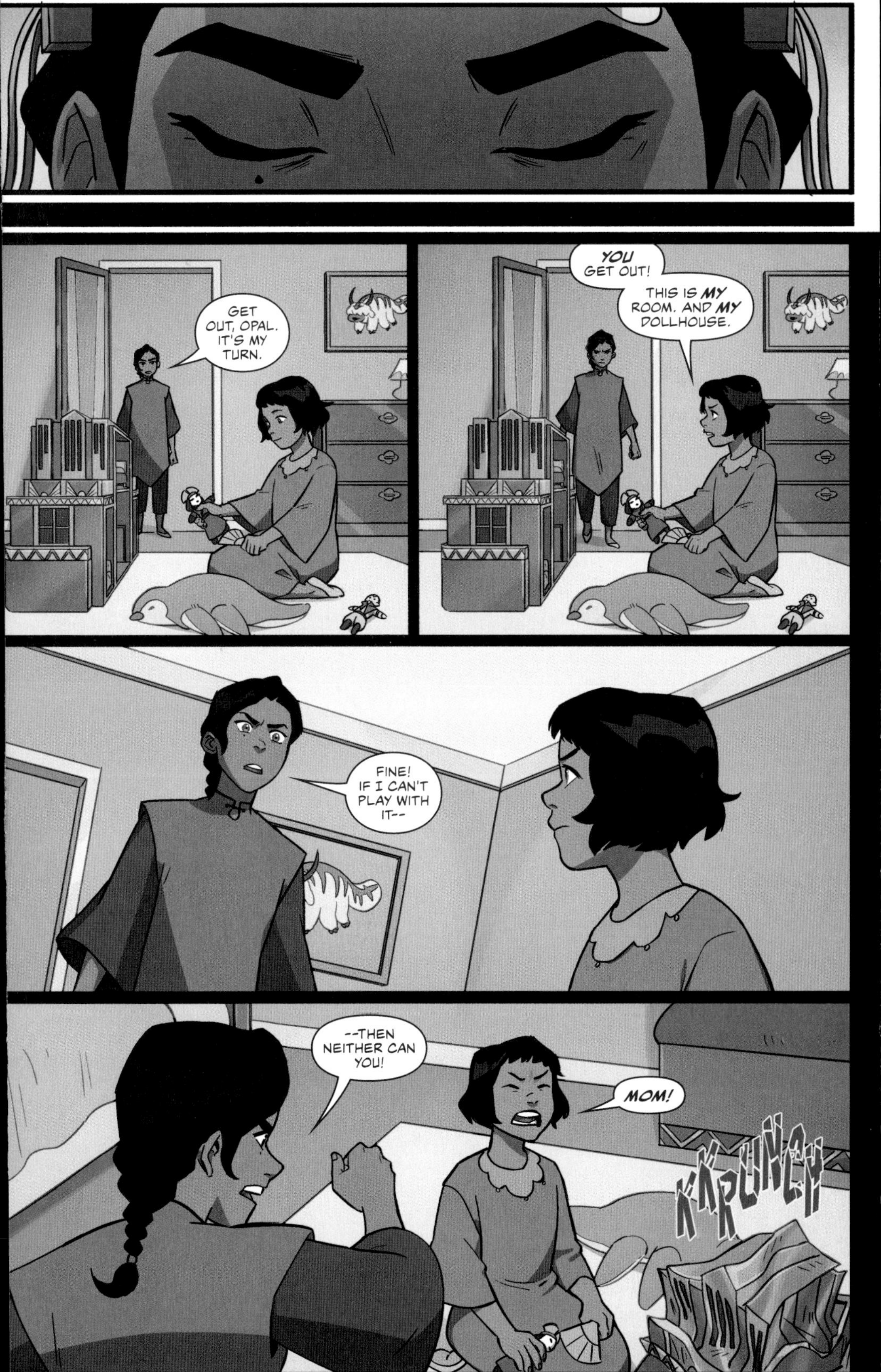
GET OUT, OPAL. IT'S MY TURN.
YOU GET OUT!
THIS IS MY ROOM. AND MY DOLLHOUSE.
FINE! IF I CAN'T PLAY WITH IT--
--THEN NEITHER CAN YOU!
MOM!
KRUNCH

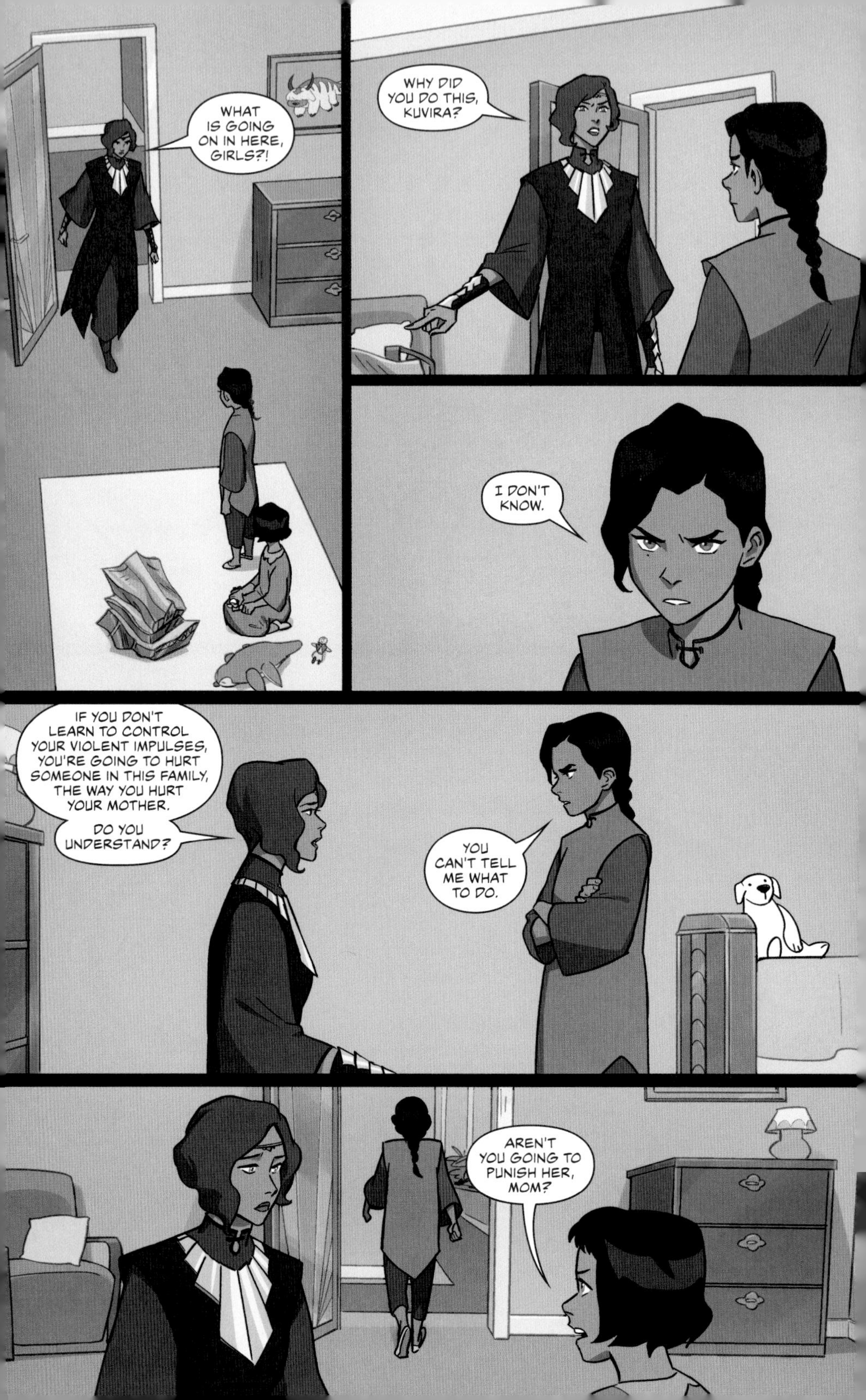
WHAT IS GOING ON IN HERE, GIRLS?!
WHY DID YOU DO THIS, KUVIRA?
I DON'T KNOW.
IF YOU DON'T LEARN TO CONTROL YOUR VIOLENT IMPULSES, YOU'RE GOING TO HURT SOMEONE IN THIS FAMILY, THE WAY YOU HURT YOUR MOTHER.
DO YOU UNDERSTAND?
YOU CAN'T TELL ME WHAT TO DO.
AREN'T YOU GOING TO PUNISH HER, MOM?

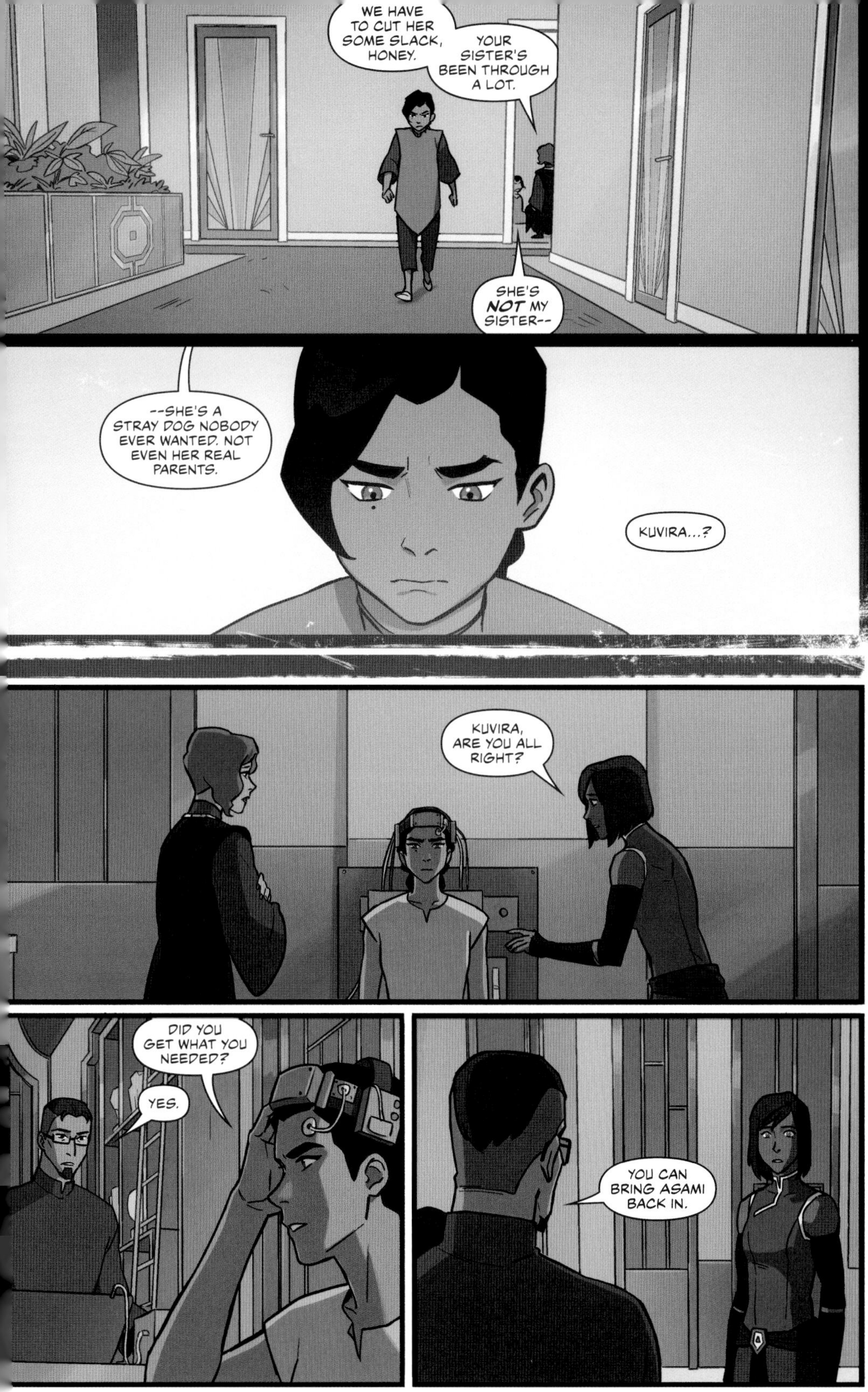

WE HAVE TO CUT HER SOME SLACK, HONEY.
YOUR SISTER'S BEEN THROUGH A LOT.
SHE'S *NOT* MY SISTER--
--SHE'S A STRAY DOG NOBODY EVER WANTED. NOT EVEN HER REAL PARENTS.
KUVIRA...?
KUVIRA, ARE YOU ALL RIGHT?
DID YOU GET WHAT YOU NEEDED?
YES.
YOU CAN BRING ASAMI BACK IN.

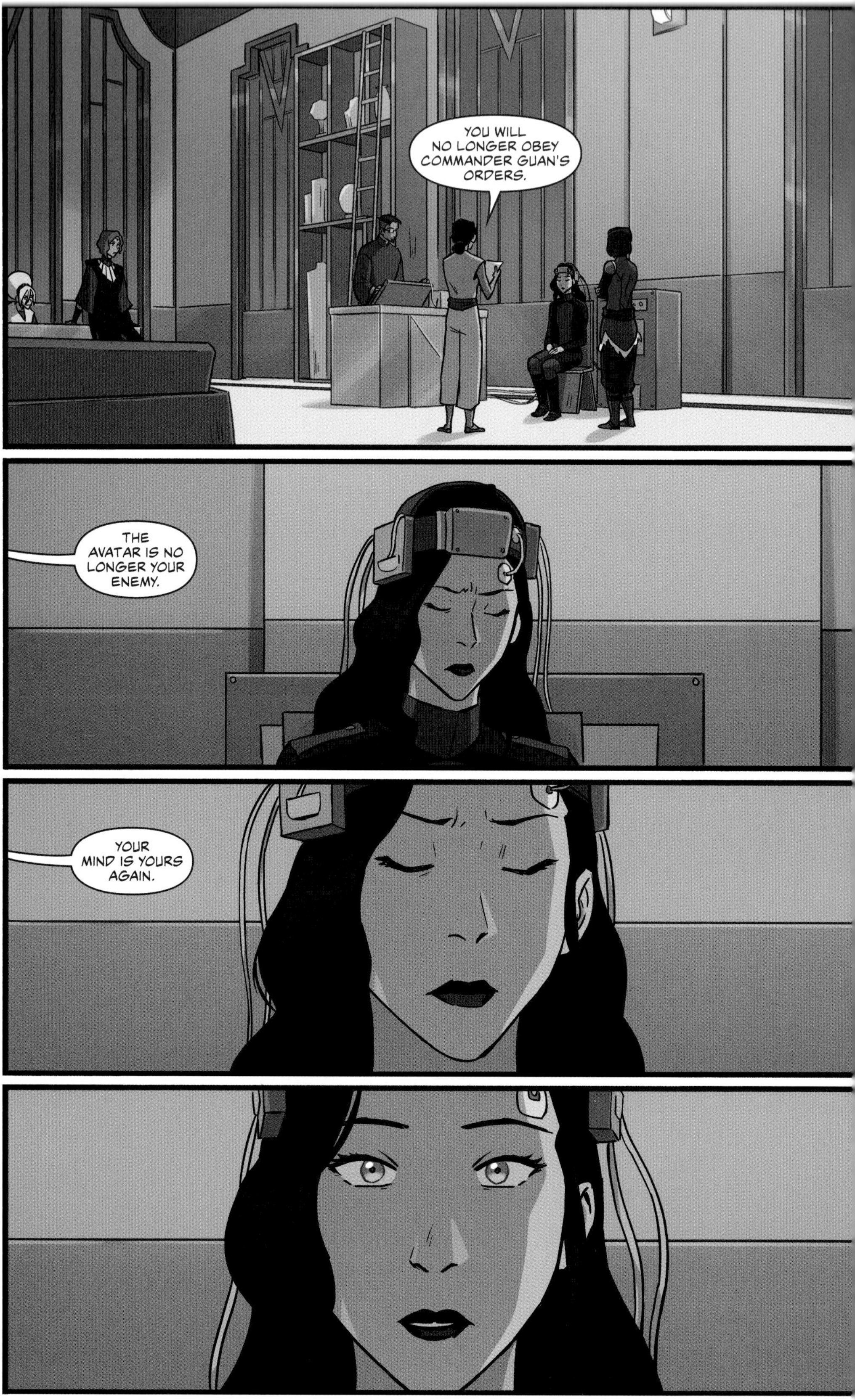
YOU WILL NO LONGER OBEY COMMANDER GUAN'S ORDERS.
THE AVATAR IS NO LONGER YOUR ENEMY.
YOUR MIND IS YOURS AGAIN.

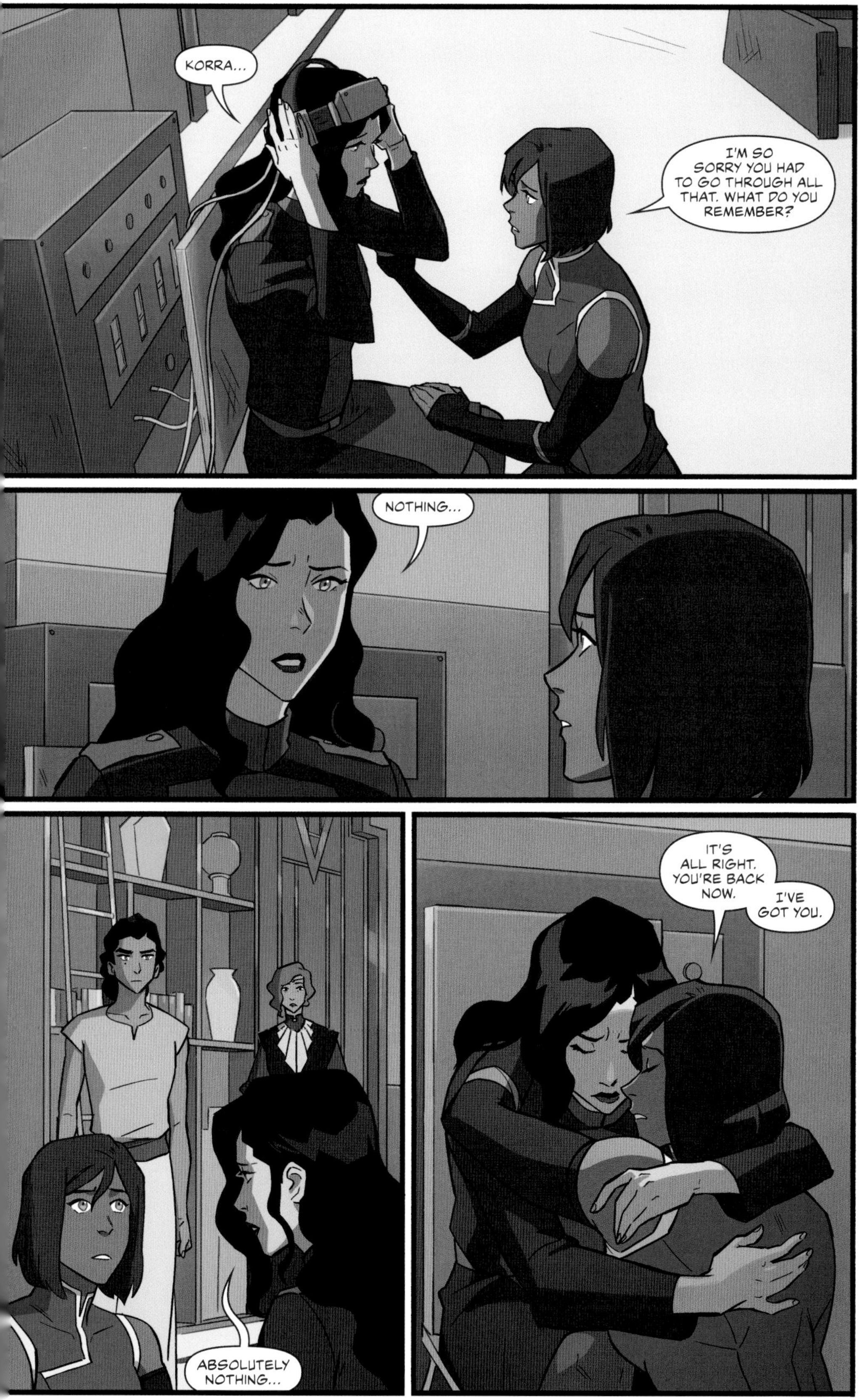
KORRA...
I'M SO SORRY YOU HAD TO GO THROUGH ALL THAT. WHAT DO YOU REMEMBER?
NOTHING...
ABSOLUTELY NOTHING...
IT'S ALL RIGHT. YOU'RE BACK NOW.
I'VE GOT YOU.

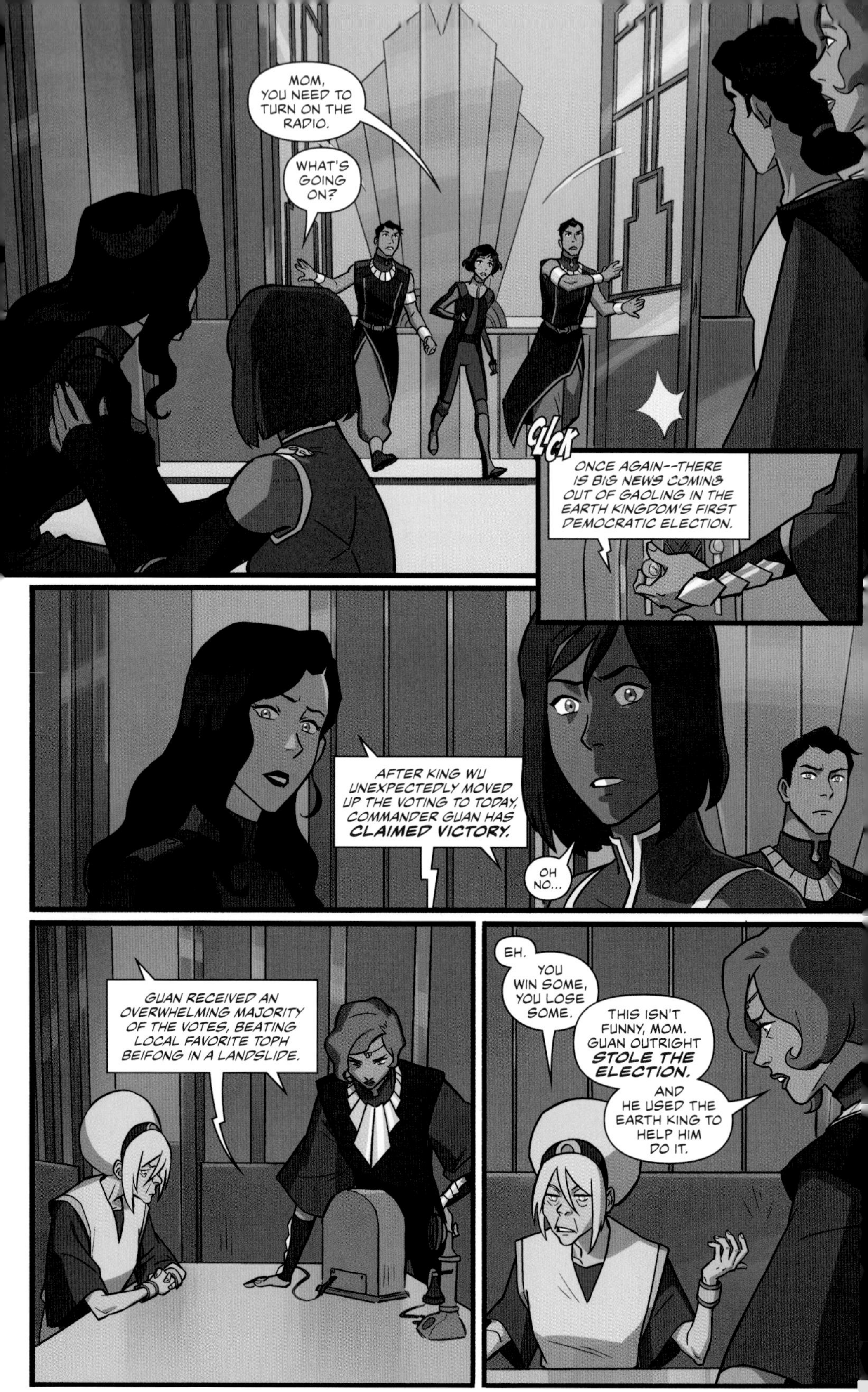
MOM, YOU NEED TO TURN ON THE RADIO.
WHAT'S GOING ON?
CLICK
ONCE AGAIN--THERE IS BIG NEWS COMING OUT OF GAOLING IN THE EARTH KINGDOM'S FIRST DEMOCRATIC ELECTION.
AFTER KING WU UNEXPECTEDLY MOVED UP THE VOTING TO TODAY, COMMANDER GUAN HAS CLAIMED VICTORY.
OH NO...
GUAN RECEIVED AN OVERWHELMING MAJORITY OF THE VOTES, BEATING LOCAL FAVORITE TOPH BEIFONG IN A LANDSLIDE.
EH.
YOU WIN SOME, YOU LOSE SOME.
THIS ISN'T FUNNY, MOM. GUAN OUTRIGHT STOLE THE ELECTION.
AND HE USED THE EARTH KING TO HELP HIM DO IT.

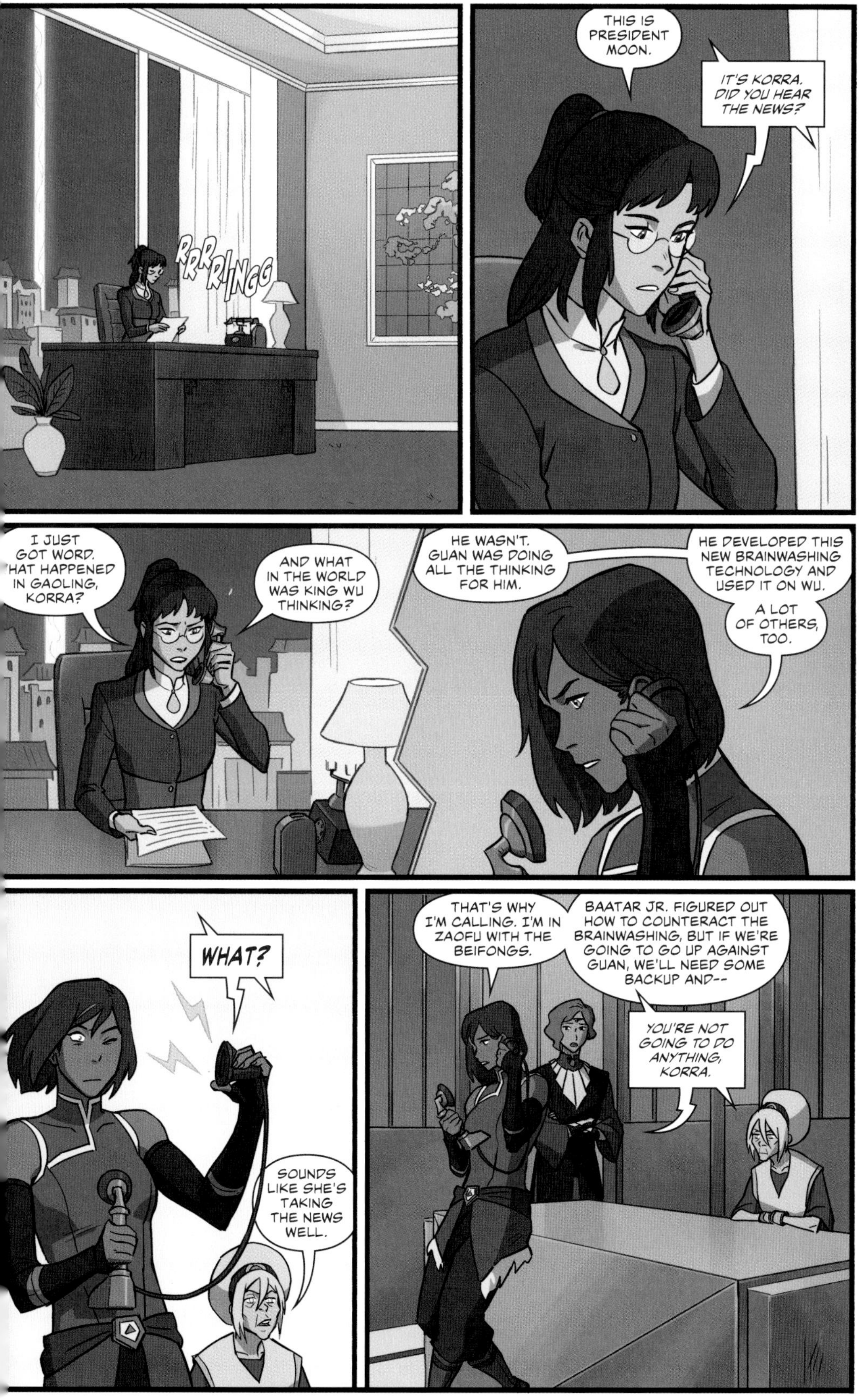
RRRRINGG
THIS IS PRESIDENT MOON.
IT'S KORRA. DID YOU HEAR THE NEWS?
I JUST GOT WORD. WHAT HAPPENED IN GAOLING, KORRA?
AND WHAT IN THE WORLD WAS KING WU THINKING?
HE WASN'T. GUAN WAS DOING ALL THE THINKING FOR HIM.
HE DEVELOPED THIS NEW BRAINWASHING TECHNOLOGY AND USED IT ON WU.
A LOT OF OTHERS, TOO.
WHAT?
SOUNDS LIKE SHE'S TAKING THE NEWS WELL.
THAT'S WHY I'M CALLING. I'M IN ZAOFU WITH THE BEIFONGS.
BAATAR JR. FIGURED OUT HOW TO COUNTERACT THE BRAINWASHING, BUT IF WE'RE GOING TO GO UP AGAINST GUAN, WE'LL NEED SOME BACKUP AND--
YOU'RE NOT GOING TO DO ANYTHING, KORRA.

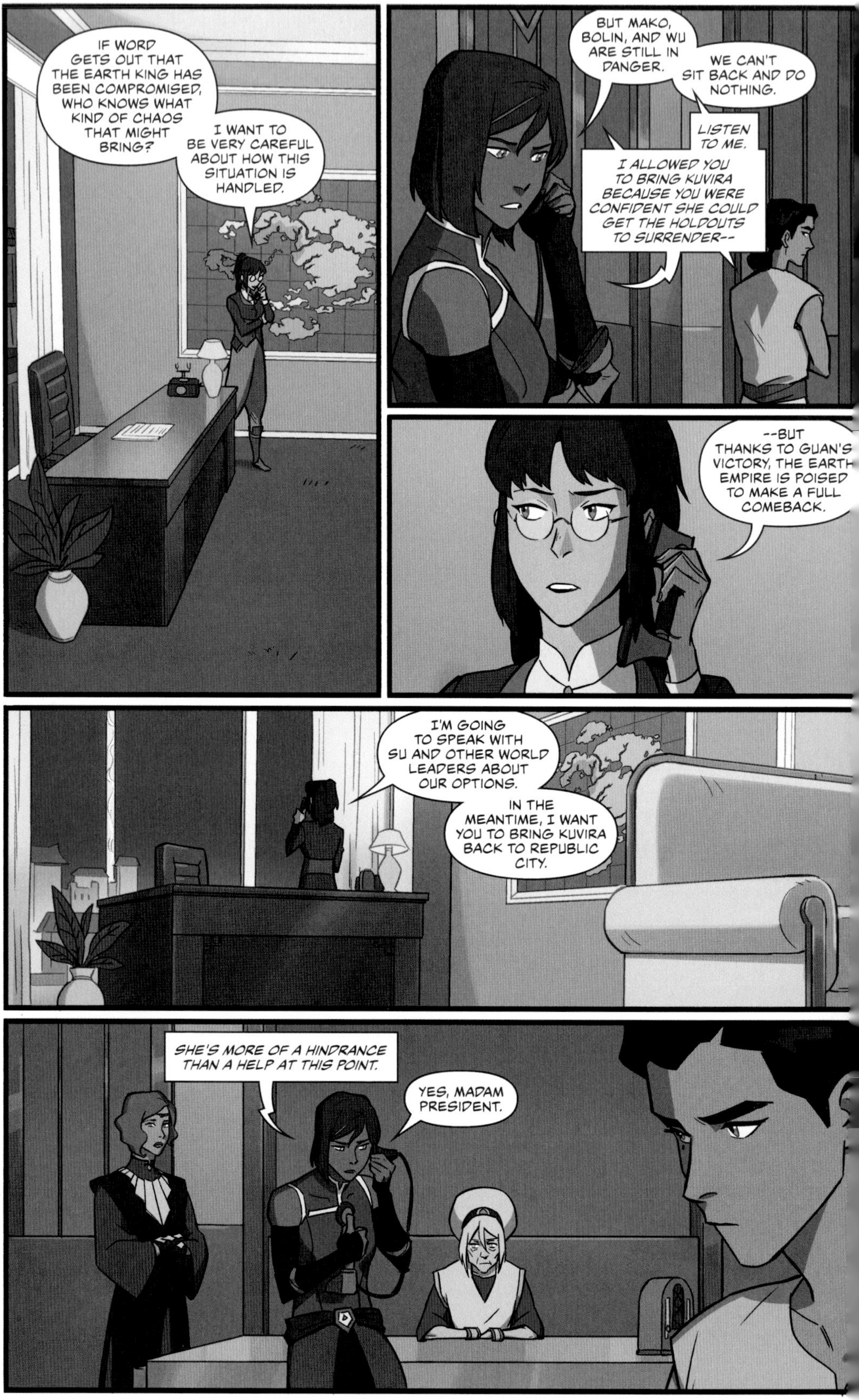
IF WORD GETS OUT THAT THE EARTH KING HAS BEEN COMPROMISED, WHO KNOWS WHAT KIND OF CHAOS THAT MIGHT BRING?
I WANT TO BE VERY CAREFUL ABOUT HOW THIS SITUATION IS HANDLED.
BUT MAKO, BOLIN, AND WU ARE STILL IN DANGER.
WE CAN'T SIT BACK AND DO NOTHING.
LISTEN TO ME.
I ALLOWED YOU TO BRING KUVIRA BECAUSE YOU WERE CONFIDENT SHE COULD GET THE HOLDOUTS TO SURRENDER--
--BUT THANKS TO GUAN'S VICTORY, THE EARTH EMPIRE IS POISED TO MAKE A FULL COMEBACK.
I'M GOING TO SPEAK WITH SU AND OTHER WORLD LEADERS ABOUT OUR OPTIONS.
IN THE MEANTIME, I WANT YOU TO BRING KUVIRA BACK TO REPUBLIC CITY.
SHE'S MORE OF A HINDRANCE THAN A HELP AT THIS POINT.
YES, MADAM PRESIDENT.

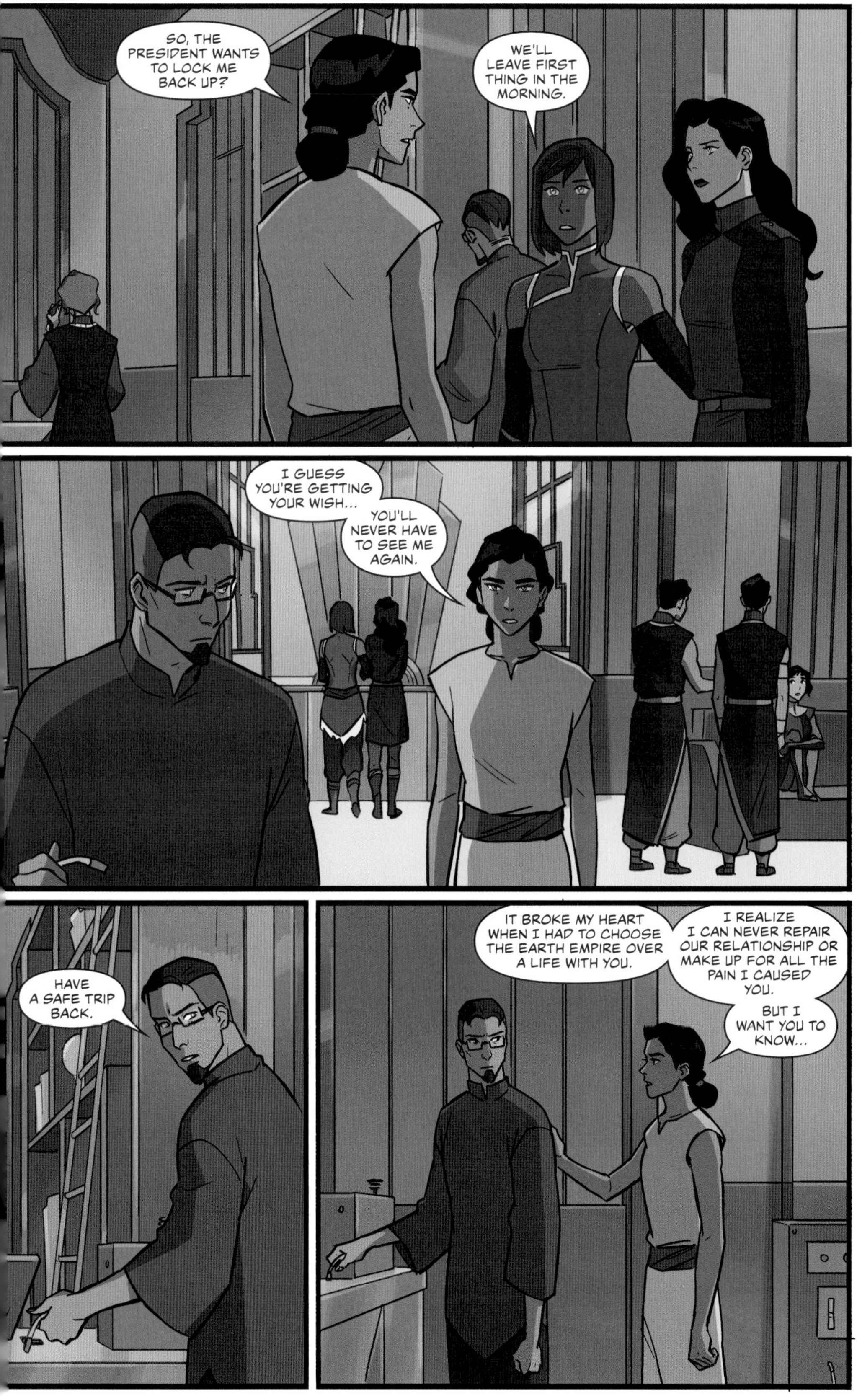
SO, THE PRESIDENT WANTS TO LOCK ME BACK UP?
WE'LL LEAVE FIRST THING IN THE MORNING.
I GUESS YOU'RE GETTING YOUR WISH...
YOU'LL NEVER HAVE TO SEE ME AGAIN.
HAVE A SAFE TRIP BACK.
IT BROKE MY HEART WHEN I HAD TO CHOOSE THE EARTH EMPIRE OVER A LIFE WITH YOU.
I REALIZE I CAN NEVER REPAIR OUR RELATIONSHIP OR MAKE UP FOR ALL THE PAIN I CAUSED YOU.
BUT I WANT YOU TO KNOW...

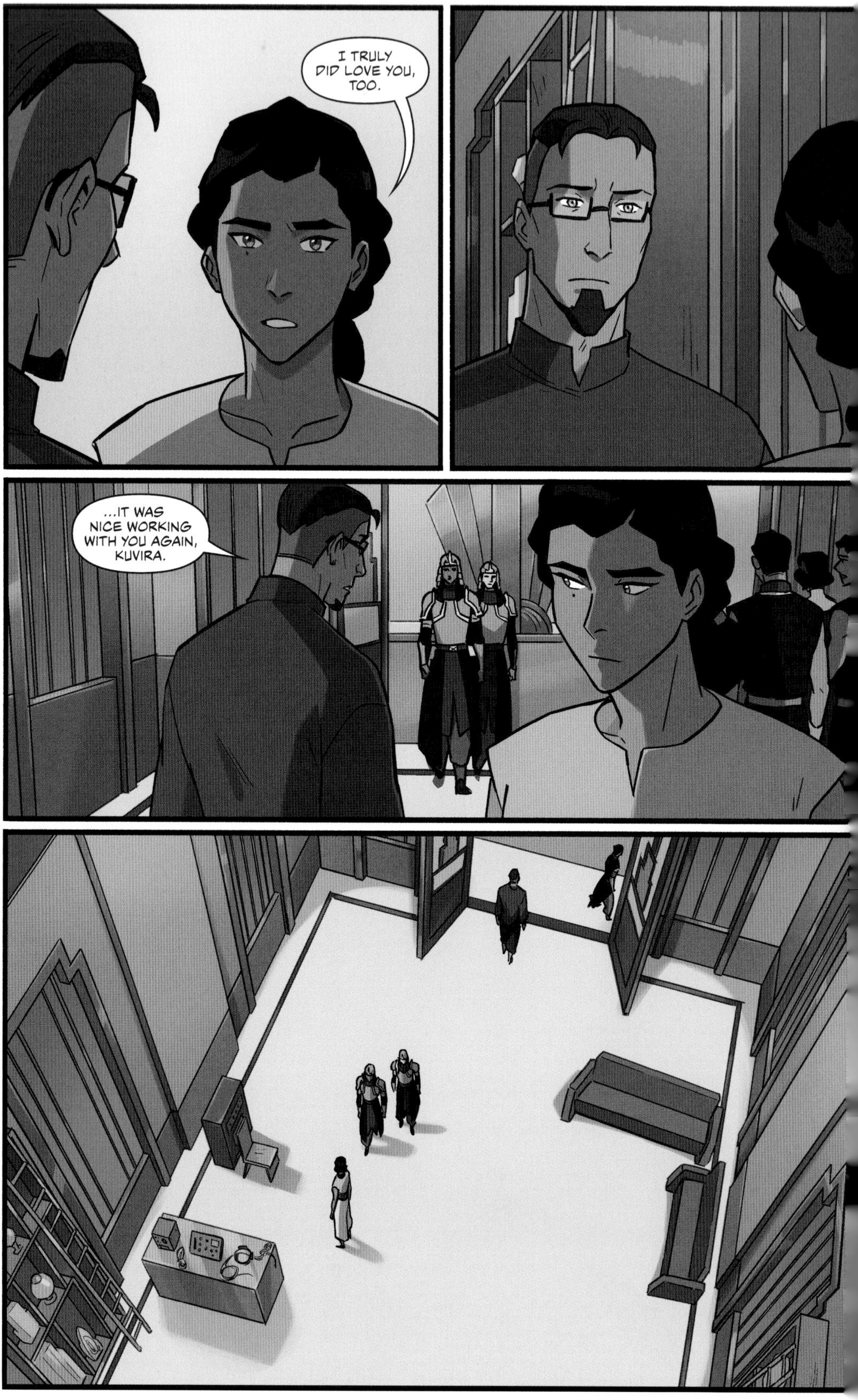
I TRULY DID LOVE YOU, TOO.
...IT WAS NICE WORKING WITH YOU AGAIN, KUVIRA.

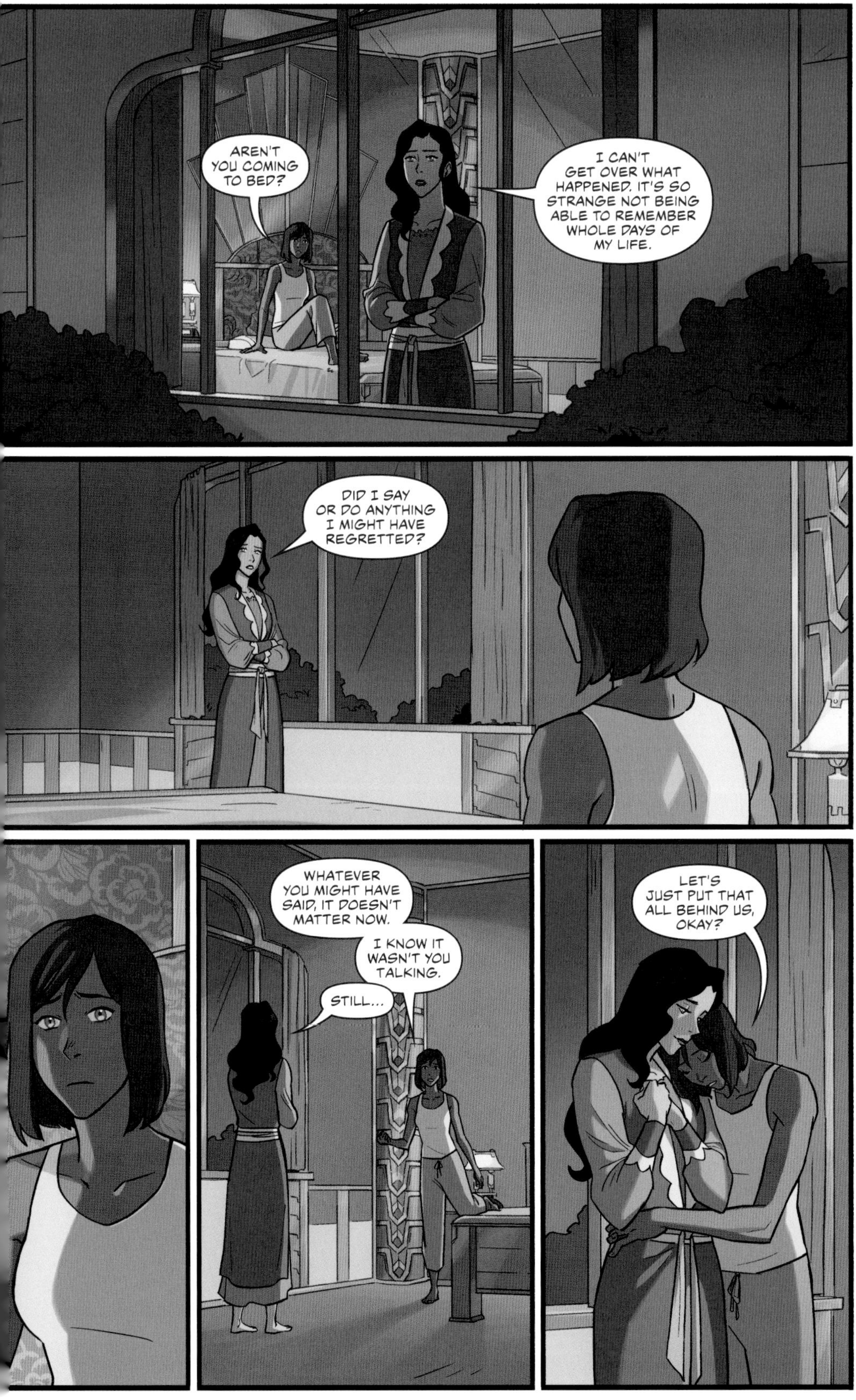
AREN'T YOU COMING TO BED?
I CAN'T GET OVER WHAT HAPPENED. IT'S SO STRANGE NOT BEING ABLE TO REMEMBER WHOLE DAYS OF MY LIFE.
DID I SAY OR DO ANYTHING I MIGHT HAVE REGRETTED?
WHATEVER YOU MIGHT HAVE SAID, IT DOESN'T MATTER NOW.
I KNOW IT WASN'T YOU TALKING.
STILL...
LET'S JUST PUT THAT ALL BEHIND US, OKAY?

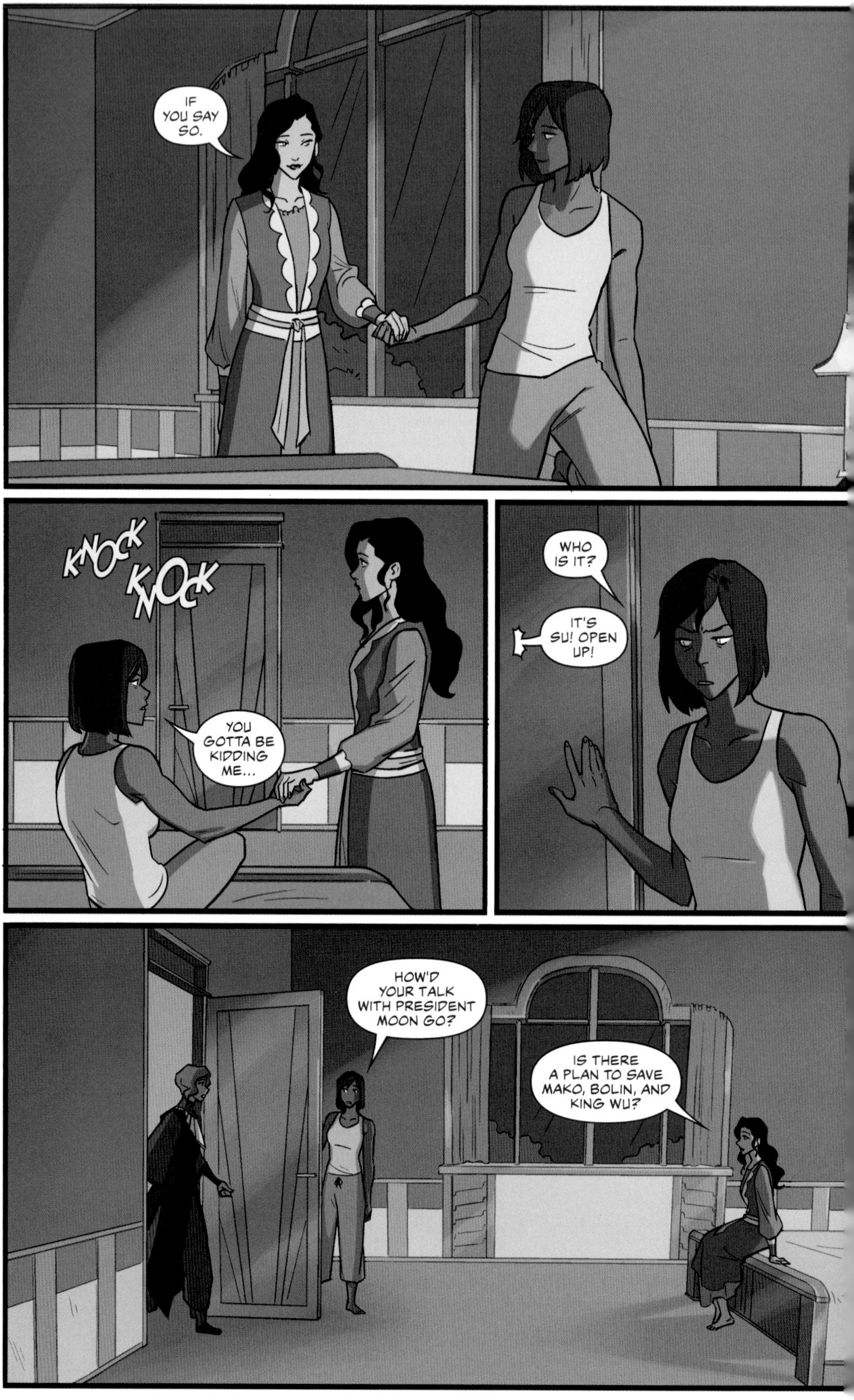
IF YOU SAY SO.
KNOCK KNOCK
YOU GOTTA BE KIDDING ME...
WHO IS IT?
IT'S SU! OPEN UP!
HOW'D YOUR TALK WITH PRESIDENT MOON GO?
IS THERE A PLAN TO SAVE MAKO, BOLIN, AND KING WU?

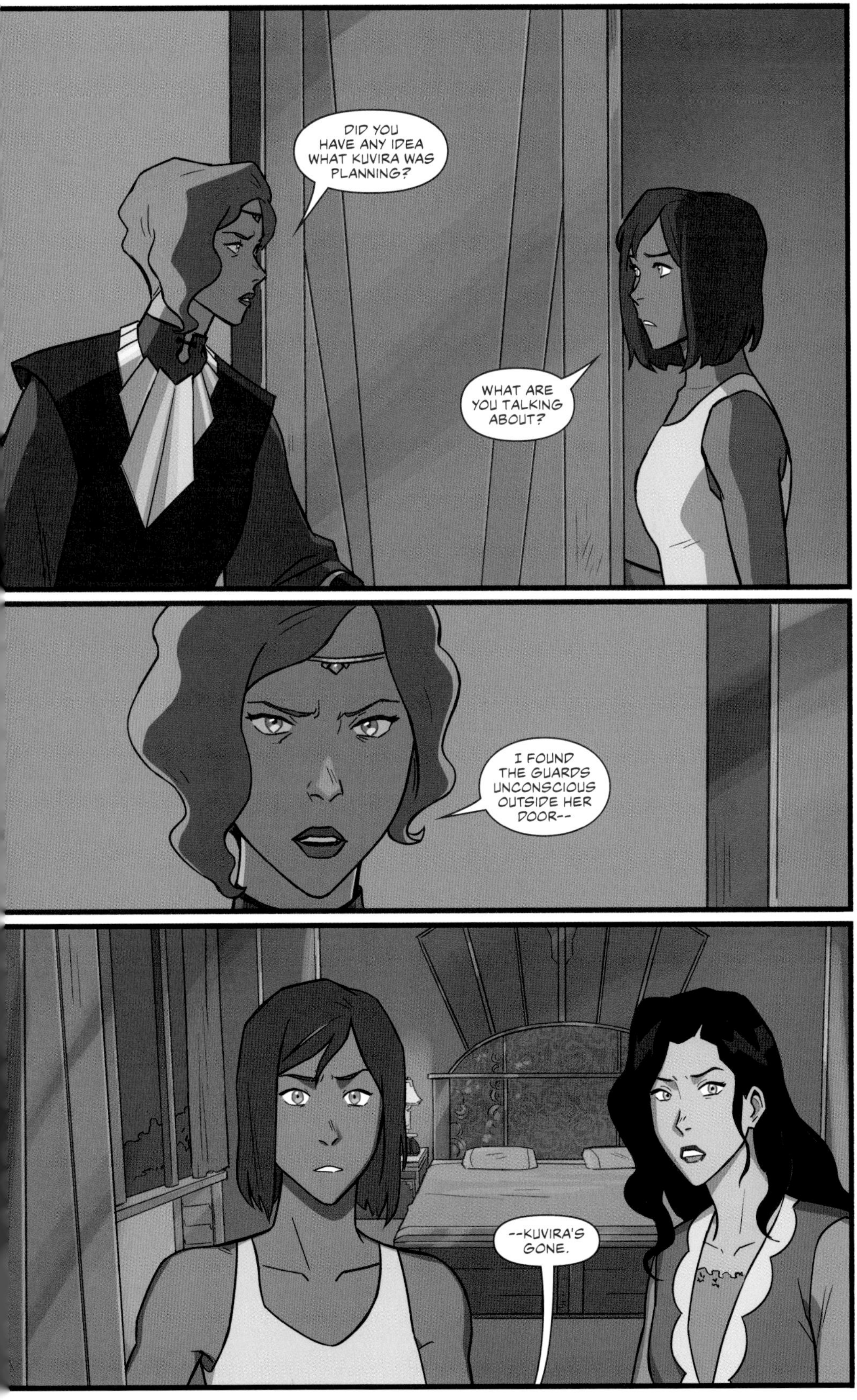
DID YOU HAVE ANY IDEA WHAT KUVIRA WAS PLANNING?
WHAT ARE YOU TALKING ABOUT?
I FOUND THE GUARDS UNCONSCIOUS OUTSIDE HER DOOR--
--KUVIRA'S GONE.

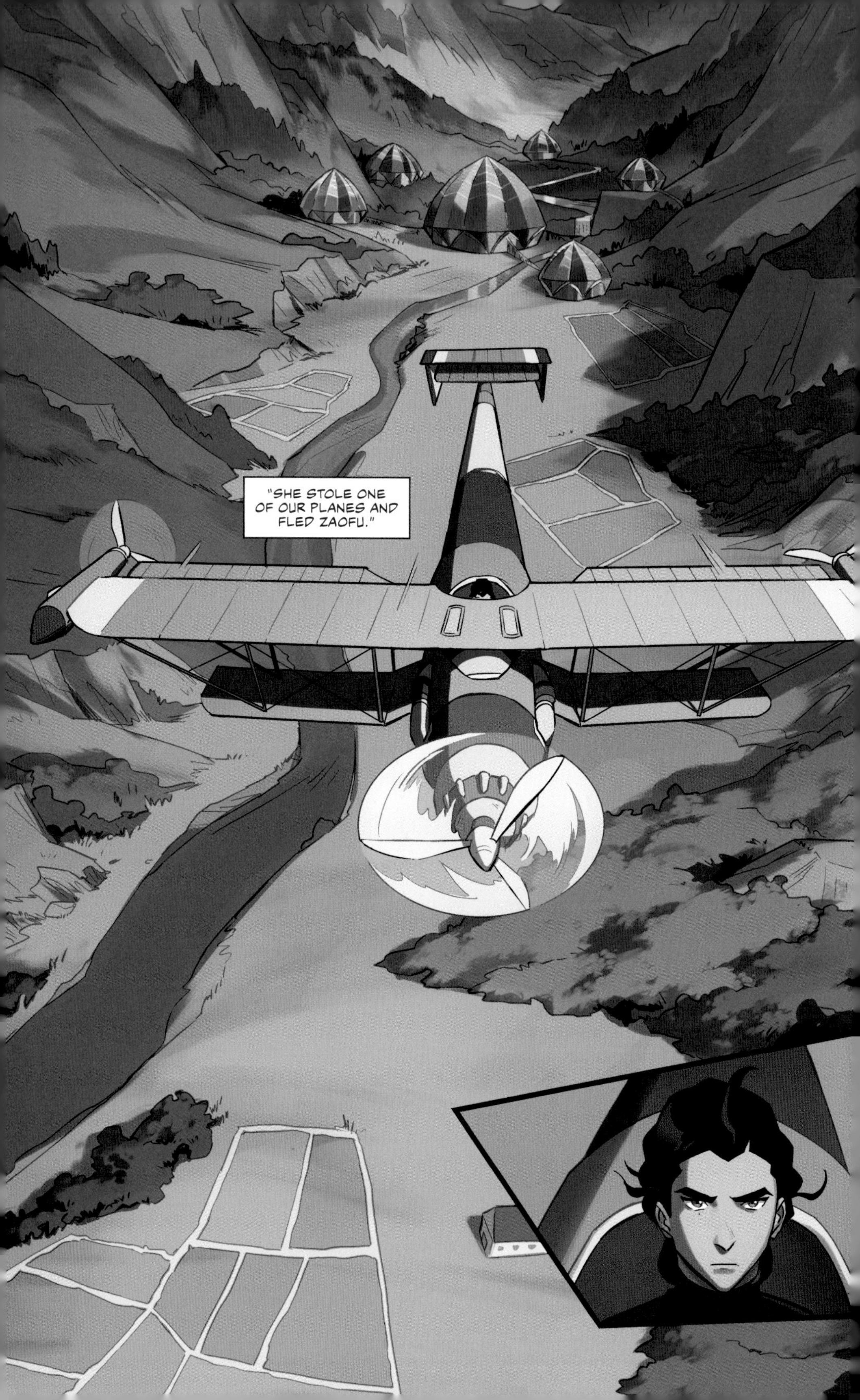
"SHE STOLE ONE OF OUR PLANES AND FLED ZAOFU."

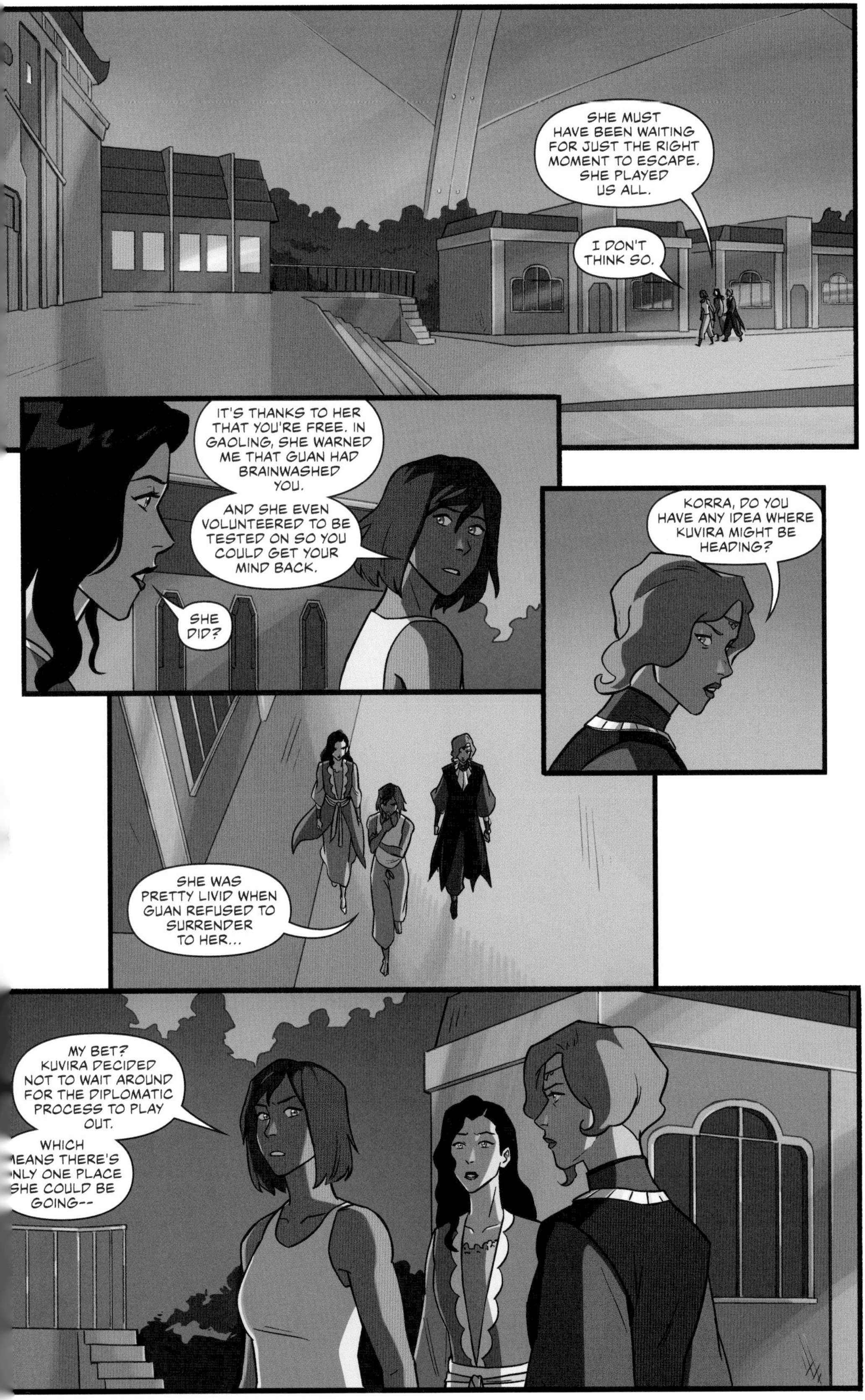
SHE MUST HAVE BEEN WAITING FOR JUST THE RIGHT MOMENT TO ESCAPE. SHE PLAYED US ALL.
I DON'T THINK SO.
IT'S THANKS TO HER THAT YOU'RE FREE. IN GAOLING, SHE WARNED ME THAT GUAN HAD BRAINWASHED YOU.
AND SHE EVEN VOLUNTEERED TO BE TESTED ON SO YOU COULD GET YOUR MIND BACK.
SHE DID?
KORRA, DO YOU HAVE ANY IDEA WHERE KUVIRA MIGHT BE HEADING?
SHE WAS PRETTY LIVID WHEN GUAN REFUSED TO SURRENDER TO HER...
MY BET? KUVIRA DECIDED NOT TO WAIT AROUND FOR THE DIPLOMATIC PROCESS TO PLAY OUT.
WHICH MEANS THERE'S ONLY ONE PLACE SHE COULD BE GOING--

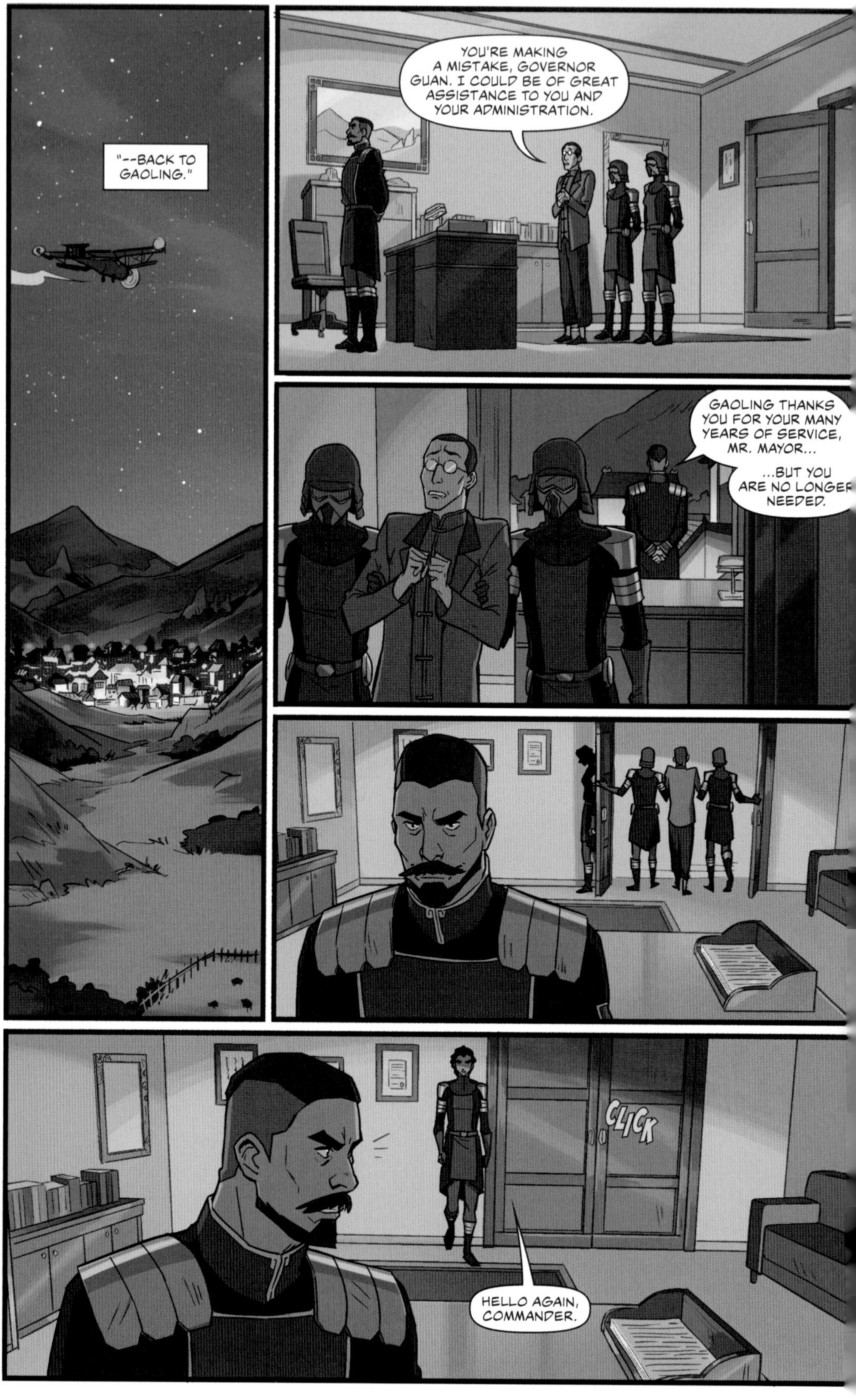
"--BACK TO GAOLING."
YOU'RE MAKING A MISTAKE, GOVERNOR GUAN. I COULD BE OF GREAT ASSISTANCE TO YOU AND YOUR ADMINISTRATION.
GAOLING THANKS YOU FOR YOUR MANY YEARS OF SERVICE, MR. MAYOR...
...BUT YOU ARE NO LONGER NEEDED.
CLICK
HELLO AGAIN, COMMANDER.

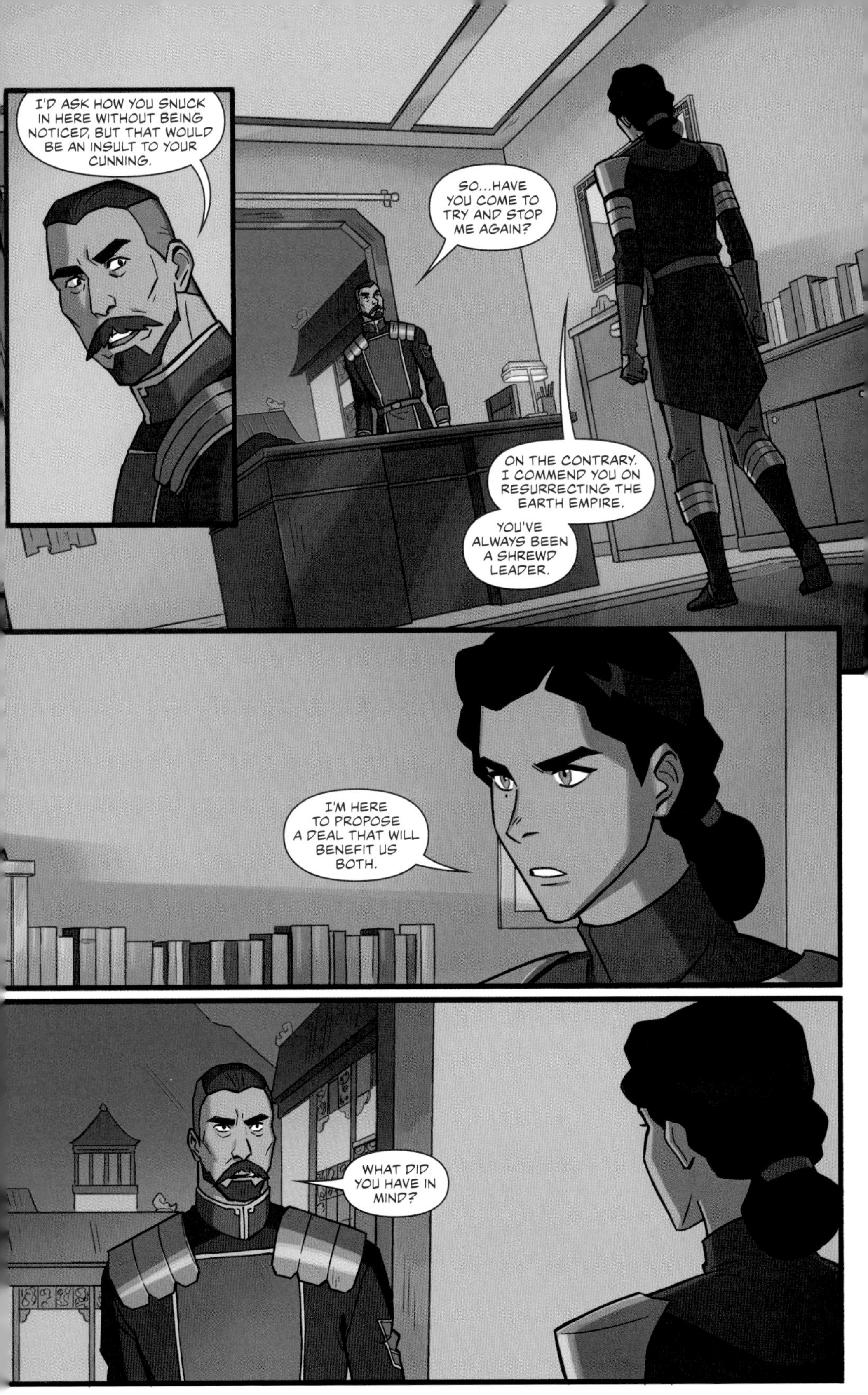
I'D ASK HOW YOU SNUCK IN HERE WITHOUT BEING NOTICED, BUT THAT WOULD BE AN INSULT TO YOUR CUNNING.
SO...HAVE YOU COME TO TRY AND STOP ME AGAIN?
ON THE CONTRARY. I COMMEND YOU ON RESURRECTING THE EARTH EMPIRE.
YOU'VE ALWAYS BEEN A SHREWD LEADER.
I'M HERE TO PROPOSE A DEAL THAT WILL BENEFIT US BOTH.
WHAT DID YOU HAVE IN MIND?

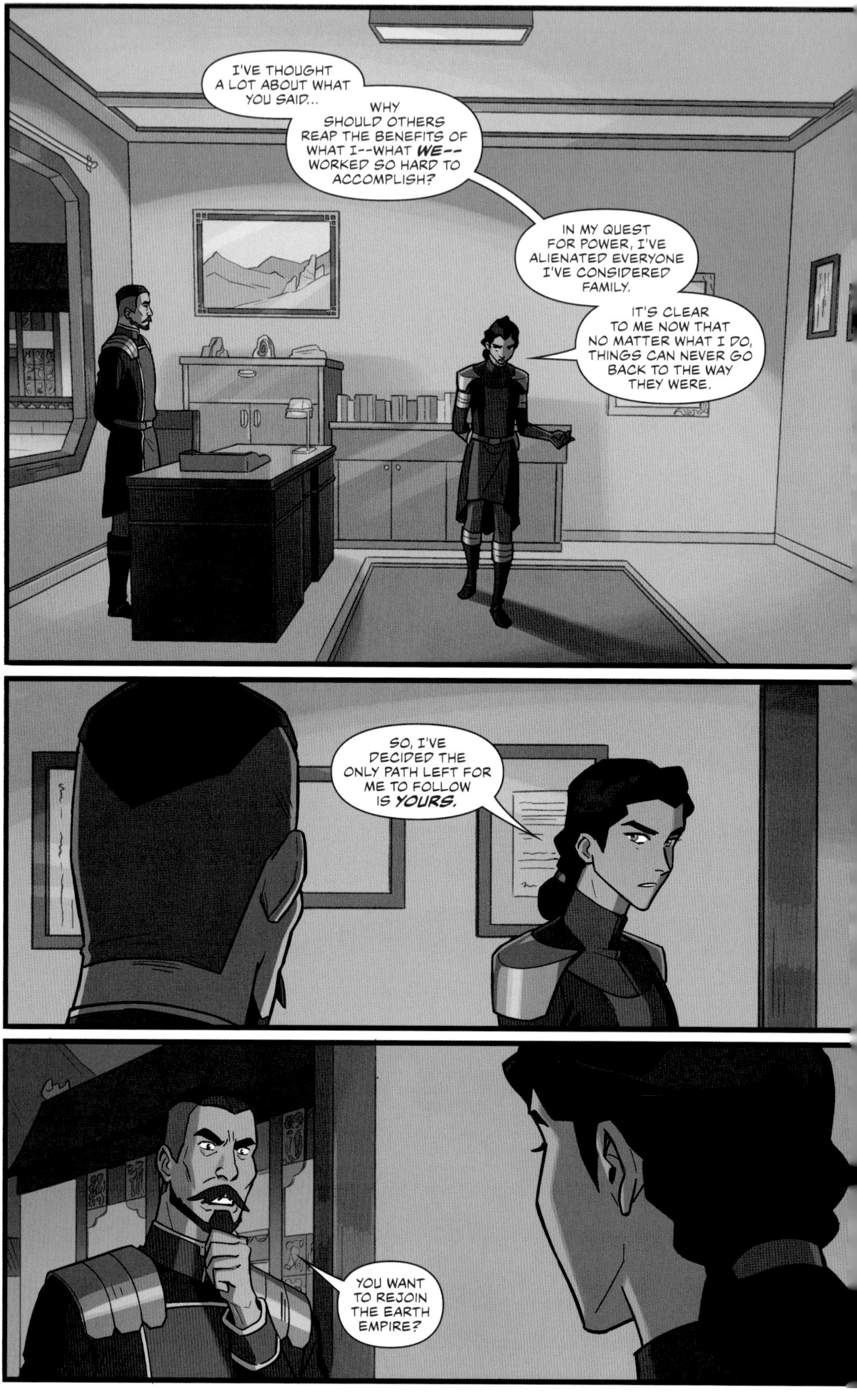
I'VE THOUGHT A LOT ABOUT WHAT YOU SAID...
WHY SHOULD OTHERS REAP THE BENEFITS OF WHAT I--WHAT *WE*--WORKED SO HARD TO ACCOMPLISH?
IN MY QUEST FOR POWER, I'VE ALIENATED EVERYONE I'VE CONSIDERED FAMILY.
IT'S CLEAR TO ME NOW THAT NO MATTER WHAT I DO, THINGS CAN NEVER GO BACK TO THE WAY THEY WERE.
SO, I'VE DECIDED THE ONLY PATH LEFT FOR ME TO FOLLOW IS *YOURS.*
YOU WANT TO REJOIN THE EARTH EMPIRE?

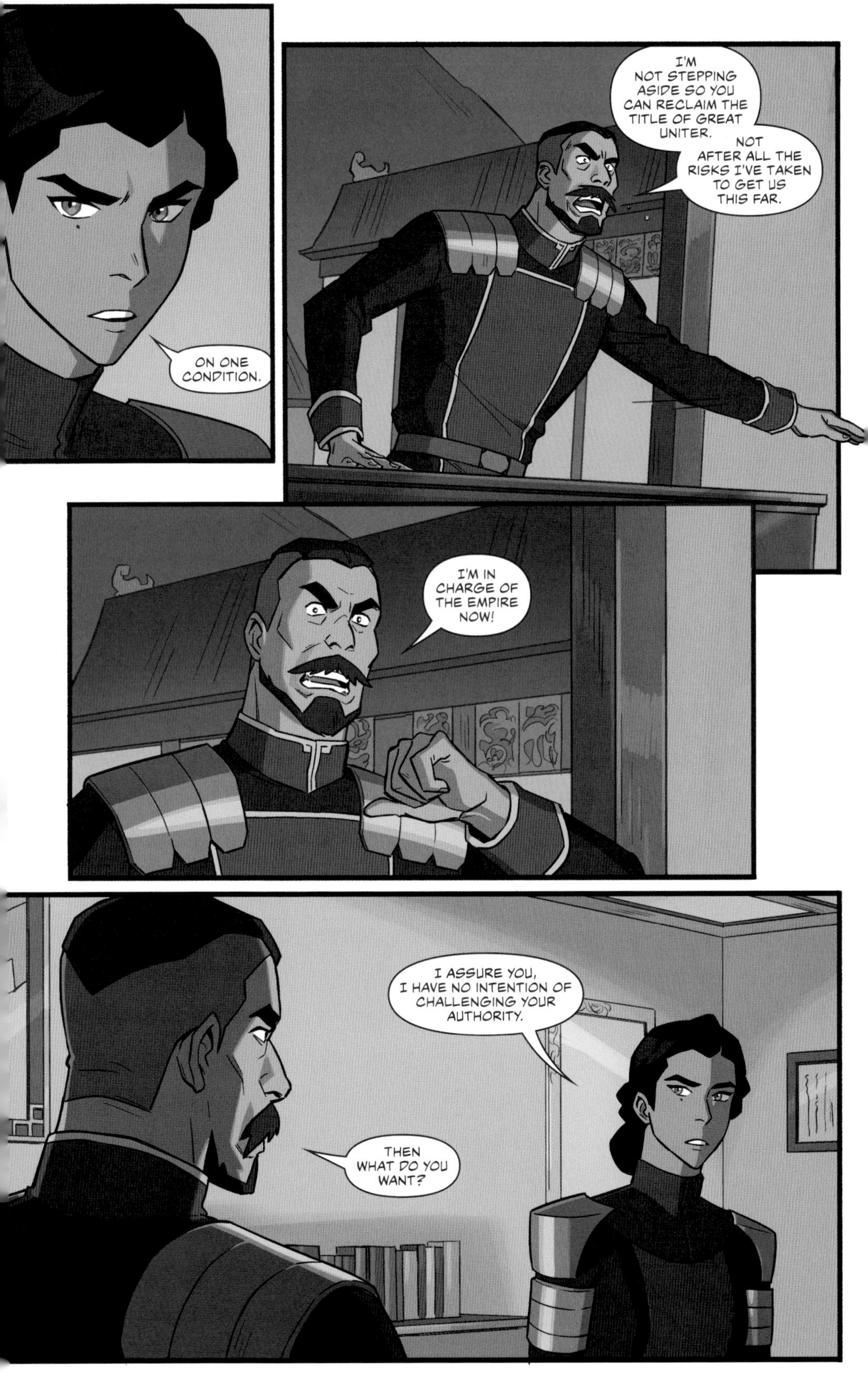
ON ONE CONDITION.
I'M NOT STEPPING ASIDE SO YOU CAN RECLAIM THE TITLE OF GREAT UNITER.
NOT AFTER ALL THE RISKS I'VE TAKEN TO GET US THIS FAR.
I'M IN CHARGE OF THE EMPIRE NOW!
I ASSURE YOU, I HAVE NO INTENTION OF CHALLENGING YOUR AUTHORITY.
THEN WHAT DO YOU WANT?

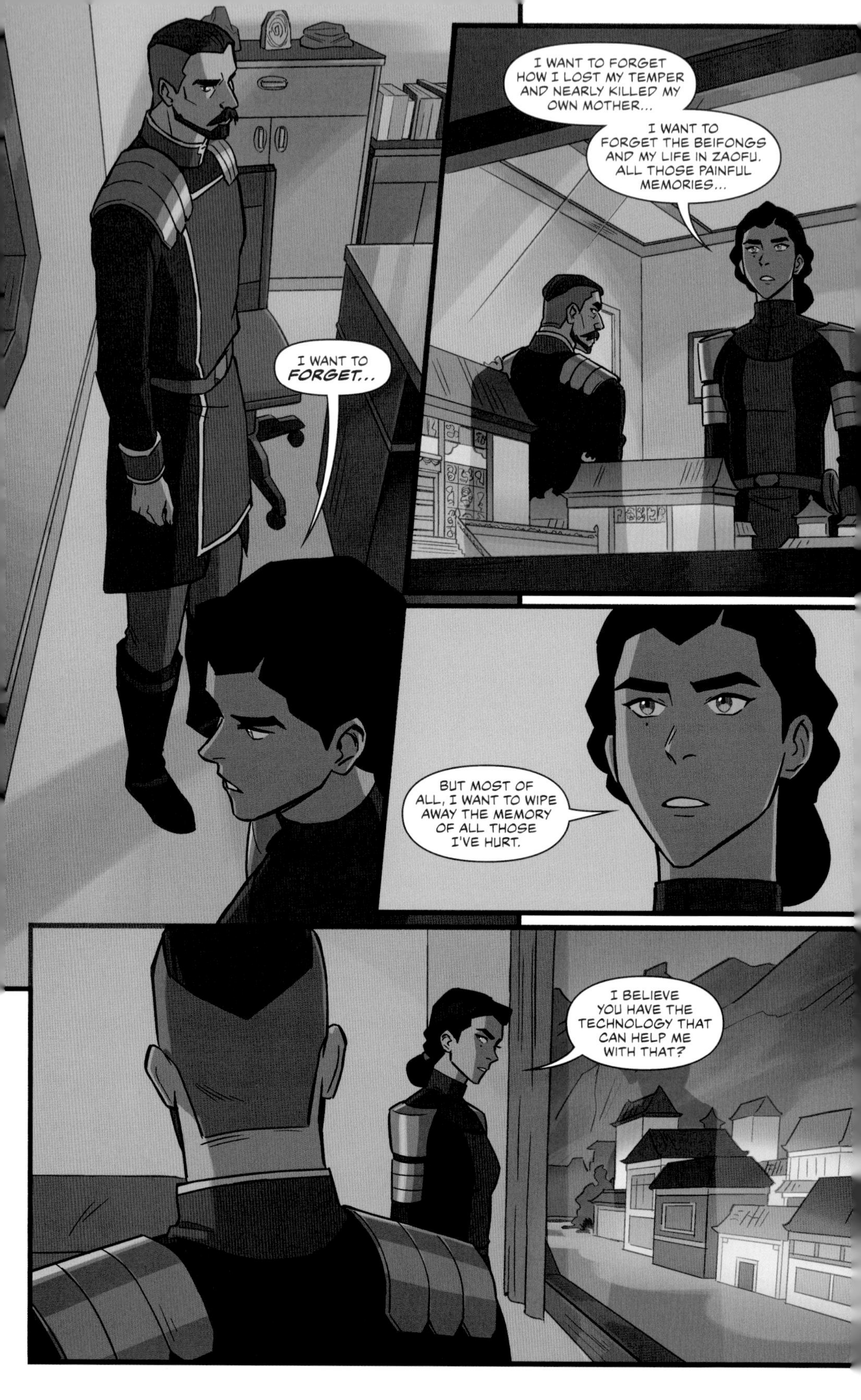
I WANT TO FORGET...
I WANT TO FORGET HOW I LOST MY TEMPER AND NEARLY KILLED MY OWN MOTHER...
I WANT TO FORGET THE BEIFONGS AND MY LIFE IN ZAOFU. ALL THOSE PAINFUL MEMORIES...
BUT MOST OF ALL, I WANT TO WIPE AWAY THE MEMORY OF ALL THOSE I'VE HURT.
I BELIEVE YOU HAVE THE TECHNOLOGY THAT CAN HELP ME WITH THAT?

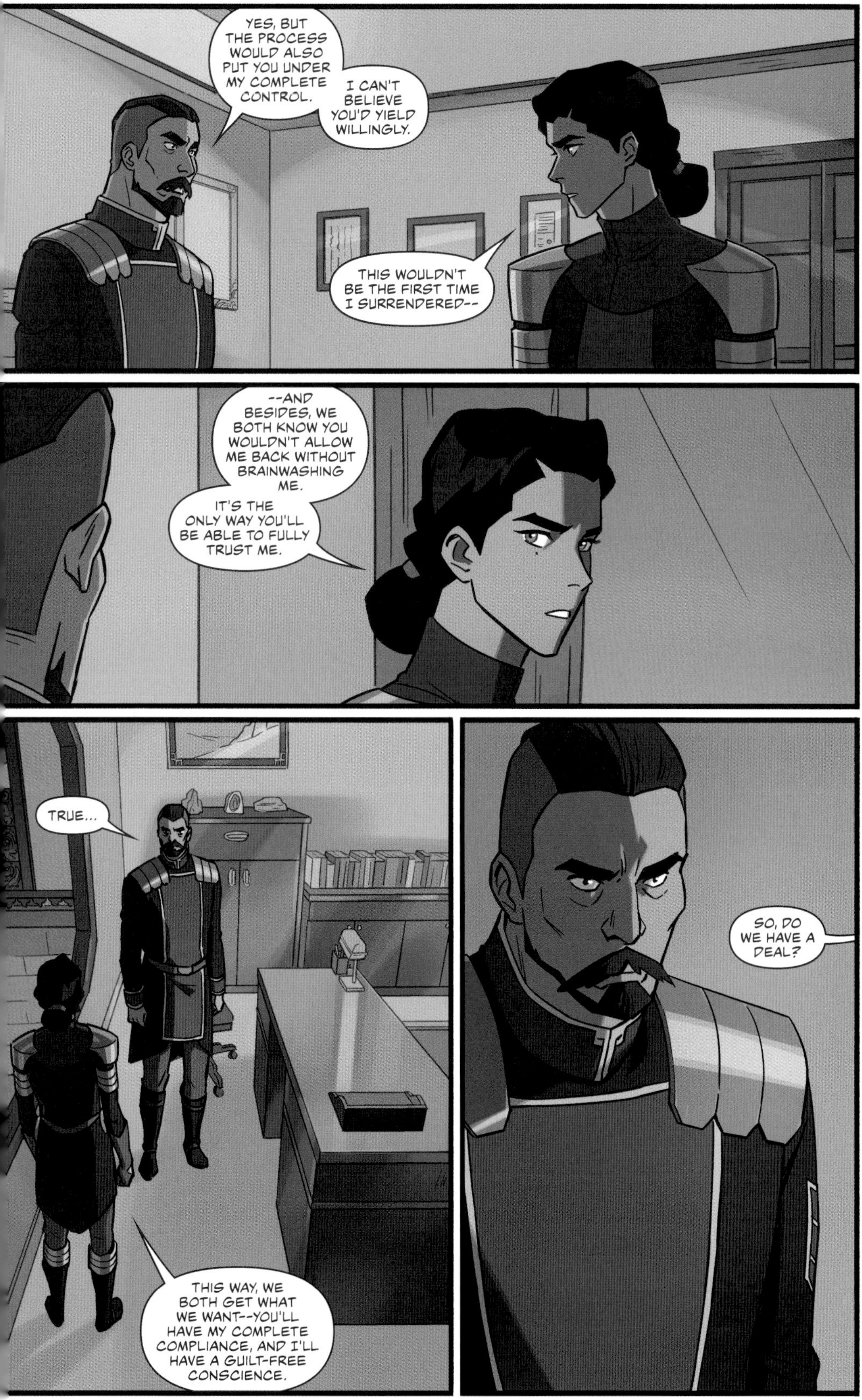
YES, BUT THE PROCESS WOULD ALSO PUT YOU UNDER MY COMPLETE CONTROL.
I CAN'T BELIEVE YOU'D YIELD WILLINGLY.
THIS WOULDN'T BE THE FIRST TIME I SURRENDERED--
--AND BESIDES, WE BOTH KNOW YOU WOULDN'T ALLOW ME BACK WITHOUT BRAINWASHING ME.
IT'S THE ONLY WAY YOU'LL BE ABLE TO FULLY TRUST ME.
TRUE...
THIS WAY, WE BOTH GET WHAT WE WANT--YOU'LL HAVE MY COMPLETE COMPLIANCE, AND I'LL HAVE A GUILT-FREE CONSCIENCE.
SO, DO WE HAVE A DEAL?

"THERE'S THE PLANE--"

--BUT NO SIGN OF KUVIRA.

JUST ADMIT IT, MOM--KUVIRA TOOK ADVANTAGE OF YOUR GOOD WILL AND BETRAYED YOU. AGAIN.

WE DON'T KNOW THAT FOR SURE. UNTIL I LEARN OTHERWISE, I'M GIVING HER THE BENEFIT OF THE DOUBT.

JUST LIKE YOU'VE ALWAYS DONE...

MAKE A PASS OVER THE CITY. I'L SEE IF I SPO HER, OPAL

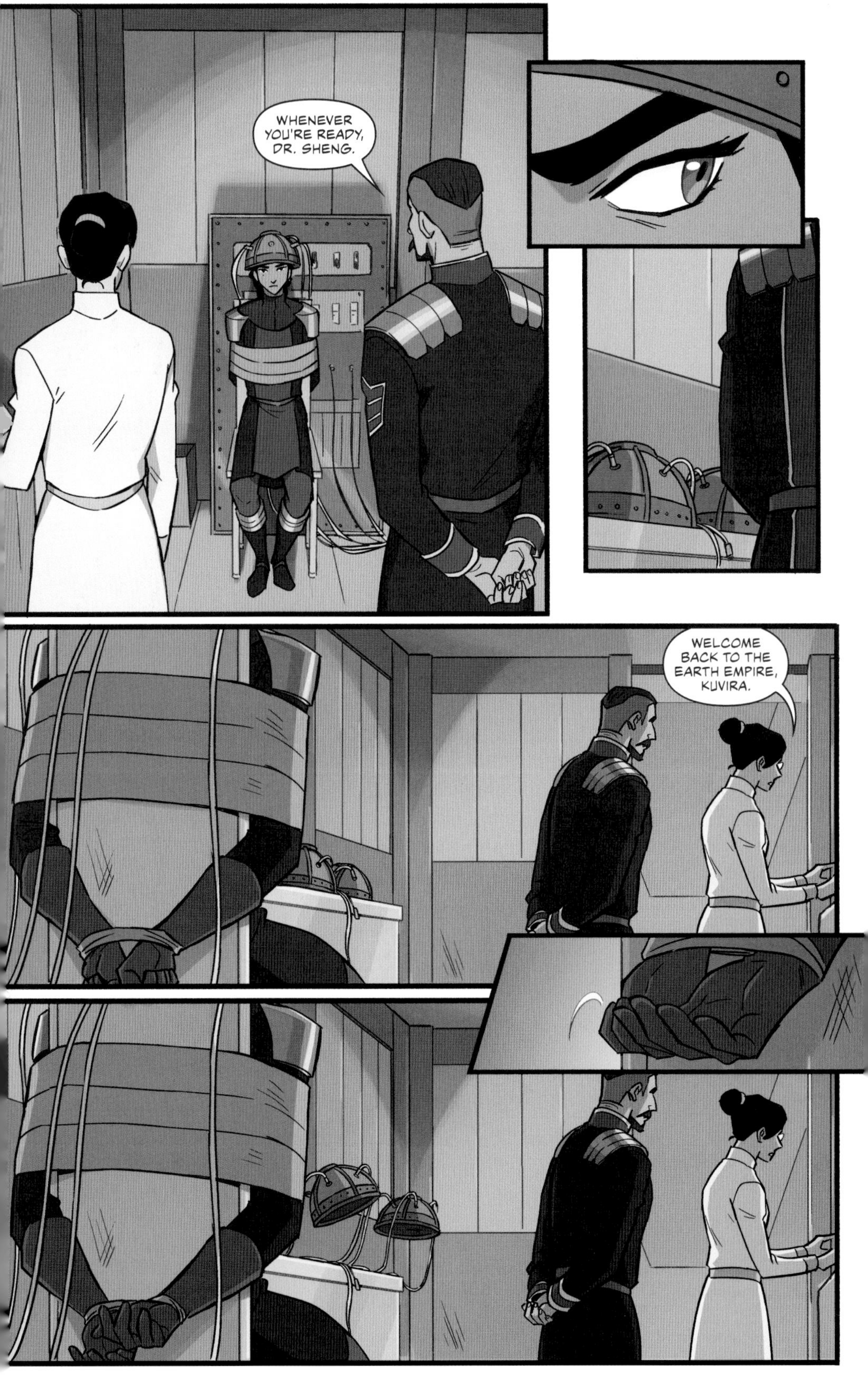
WHENEVER YOU'RE READY, DR. SHENG.
WELCOME BACK TO THE EARTH EMPIRE, KUVIRA.

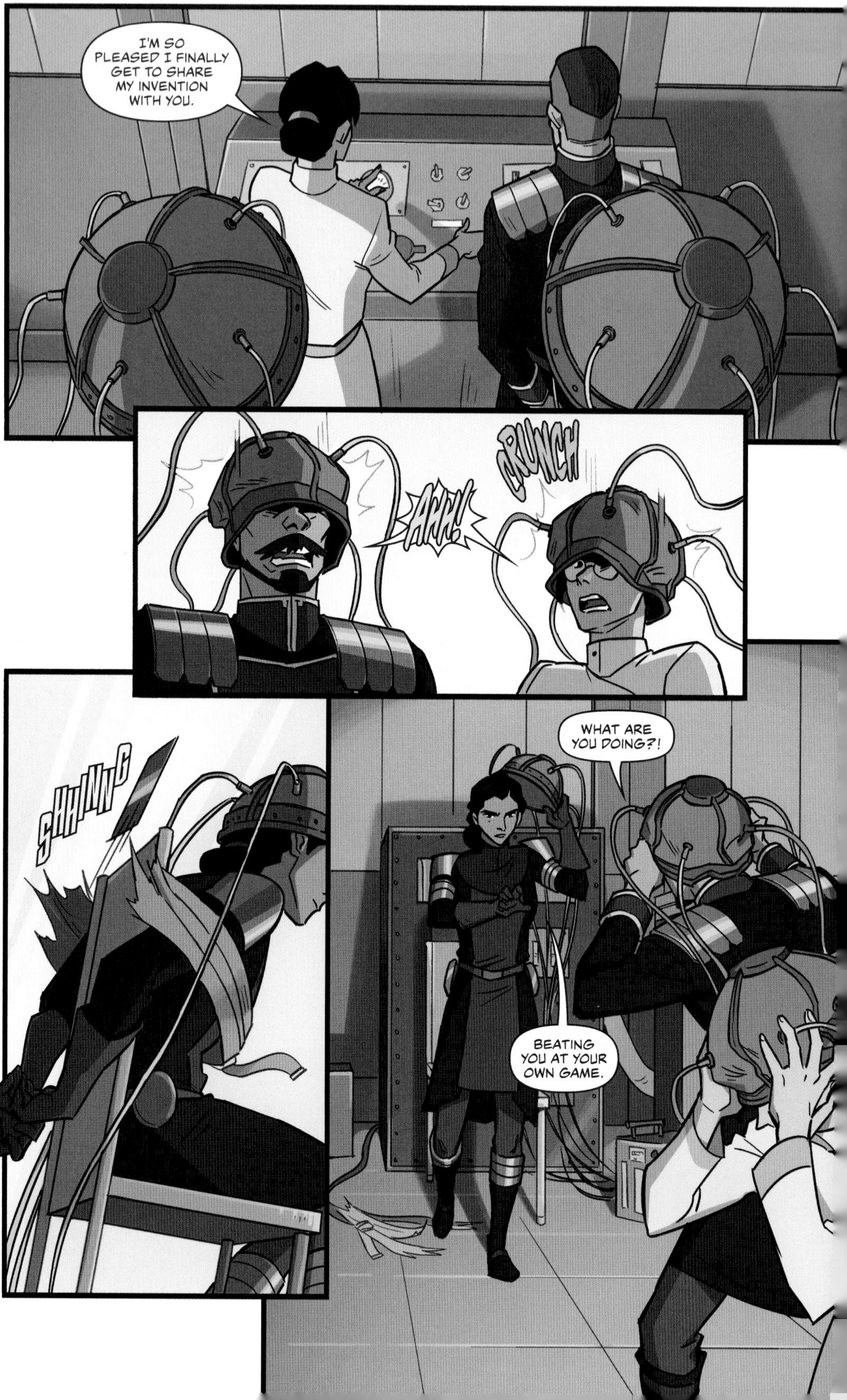
I'M SO PLEASED I FINALLY GET TO SHARE MY INVENTION WITH YOU.
CRUNCH
AHH!
SHHINNG
WHAT ARE YOU DOING?!
BEATING YOU AT YOUR OWN GAME.

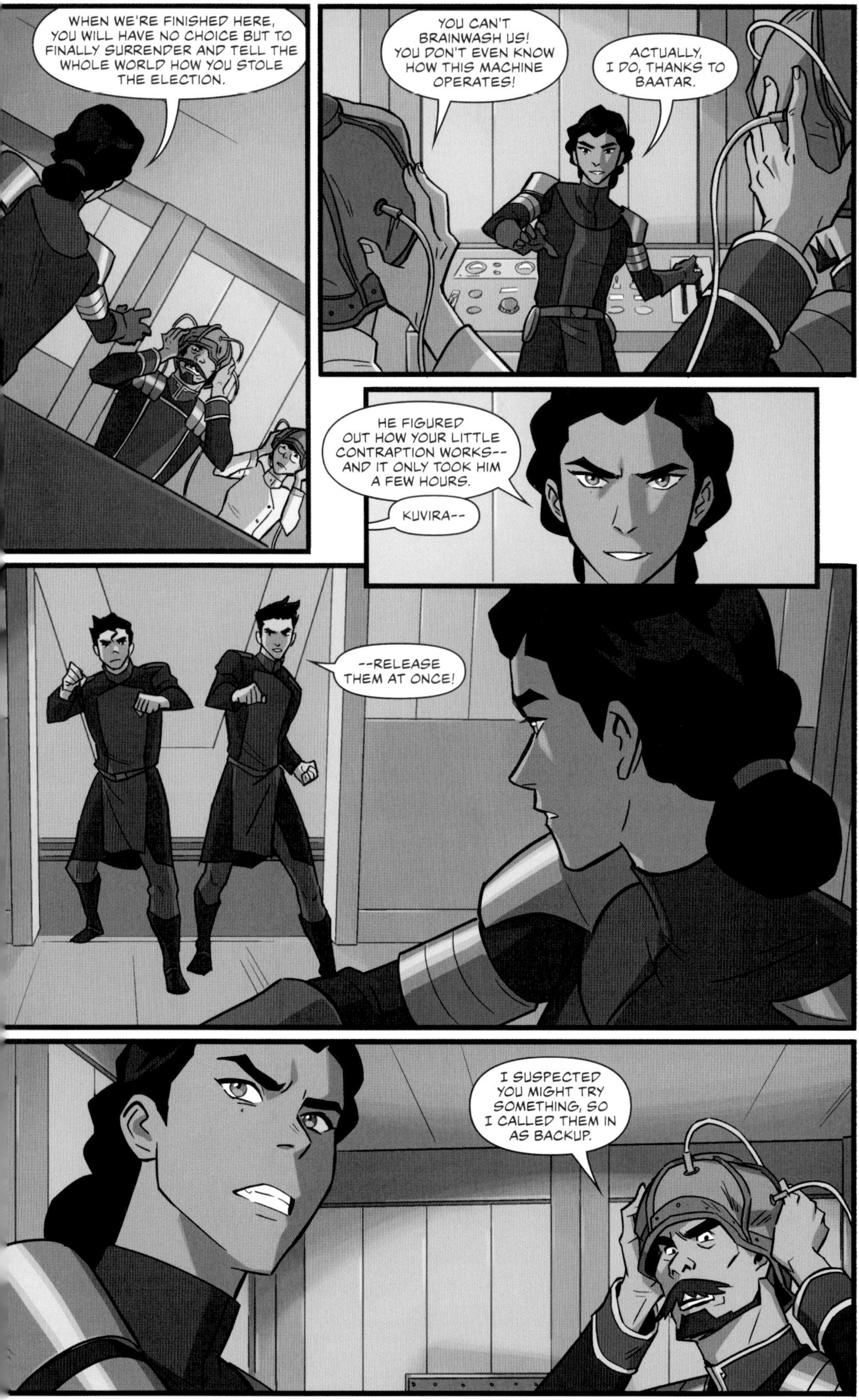
WHEN WE'RE FINISHED HERE, YOU WILL HAVE NO CHOICE BUT TO FINALLY SURRENDER AND TELL THE WHOLE WORLD HOW YOU STOLE THE ELECTION.
YOU CAN'T BRAINWASH US! YOU DON'T EVEN KNOW HOW THIS MACHINE OPERATES!
ACTUALLY, I DO, THANKS TO BAATAR.
HE FIGURED OUT HOW YOUR LITTLE CONTRAPTION WORKS-- AND IT ONLY TOOK HIM A FEW HOURS.
KUVIRA--
--RELEASE THEM AT ONCE!
I SUSPECTED YOU MIGHT TRY SOMETHING, SO I CALLED THEM IN AS BACKUP.

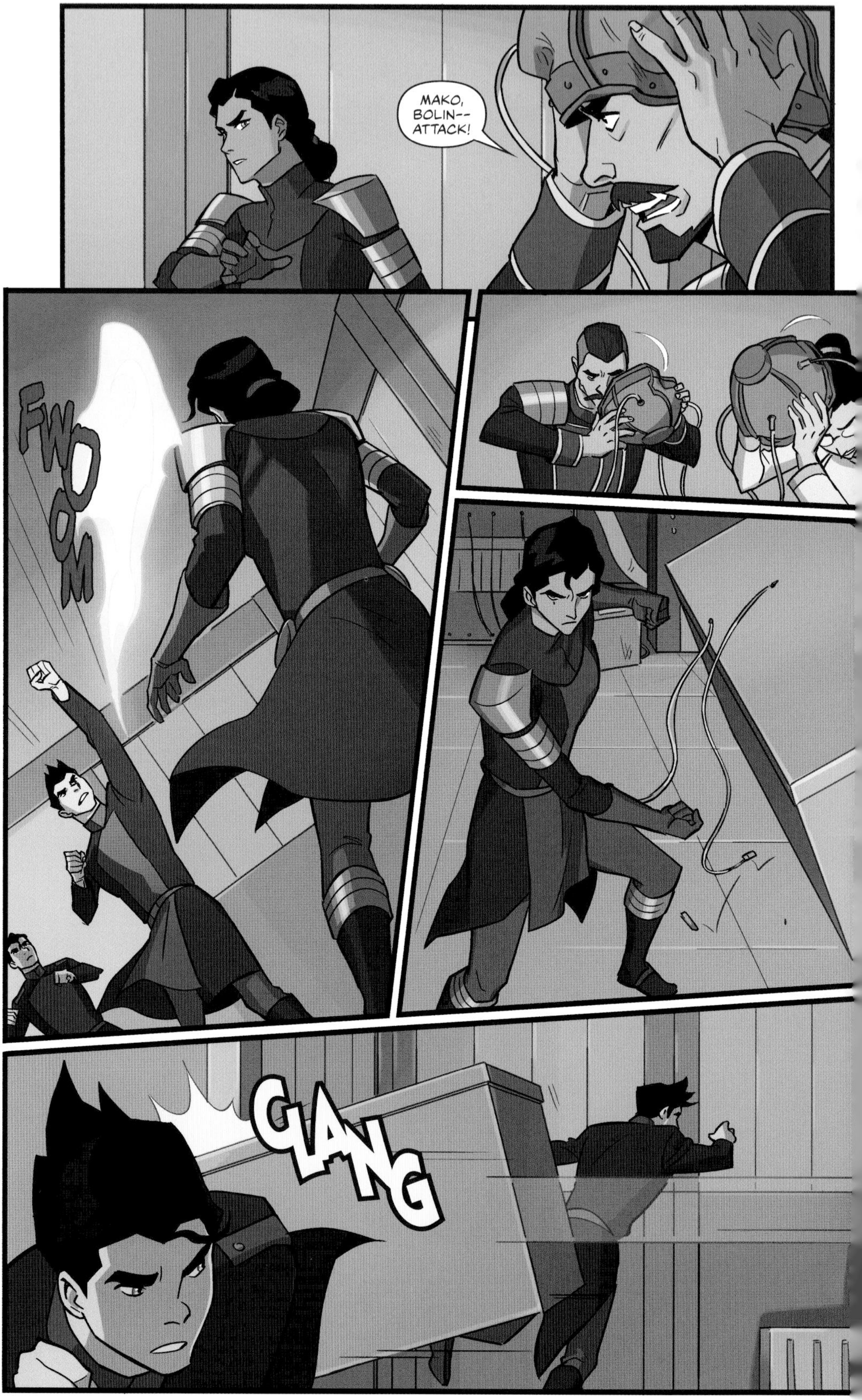
MAKO, BOLIN-- ATTACK!
FWOOM
CLANG

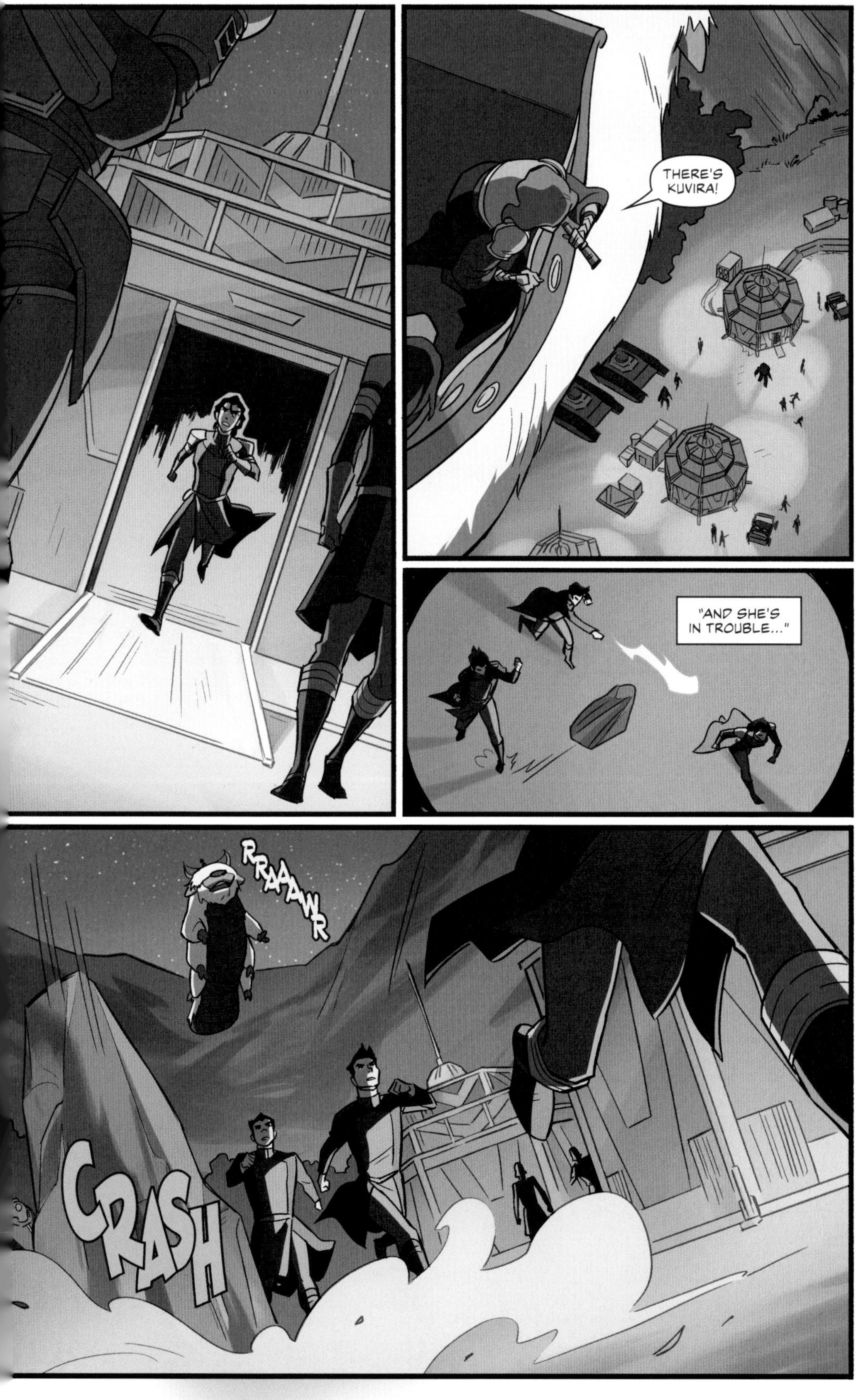
THERE'S KUVIRA!
"AND SHE'S IN TROUBLE..."
RRAAAAWR
CRASH

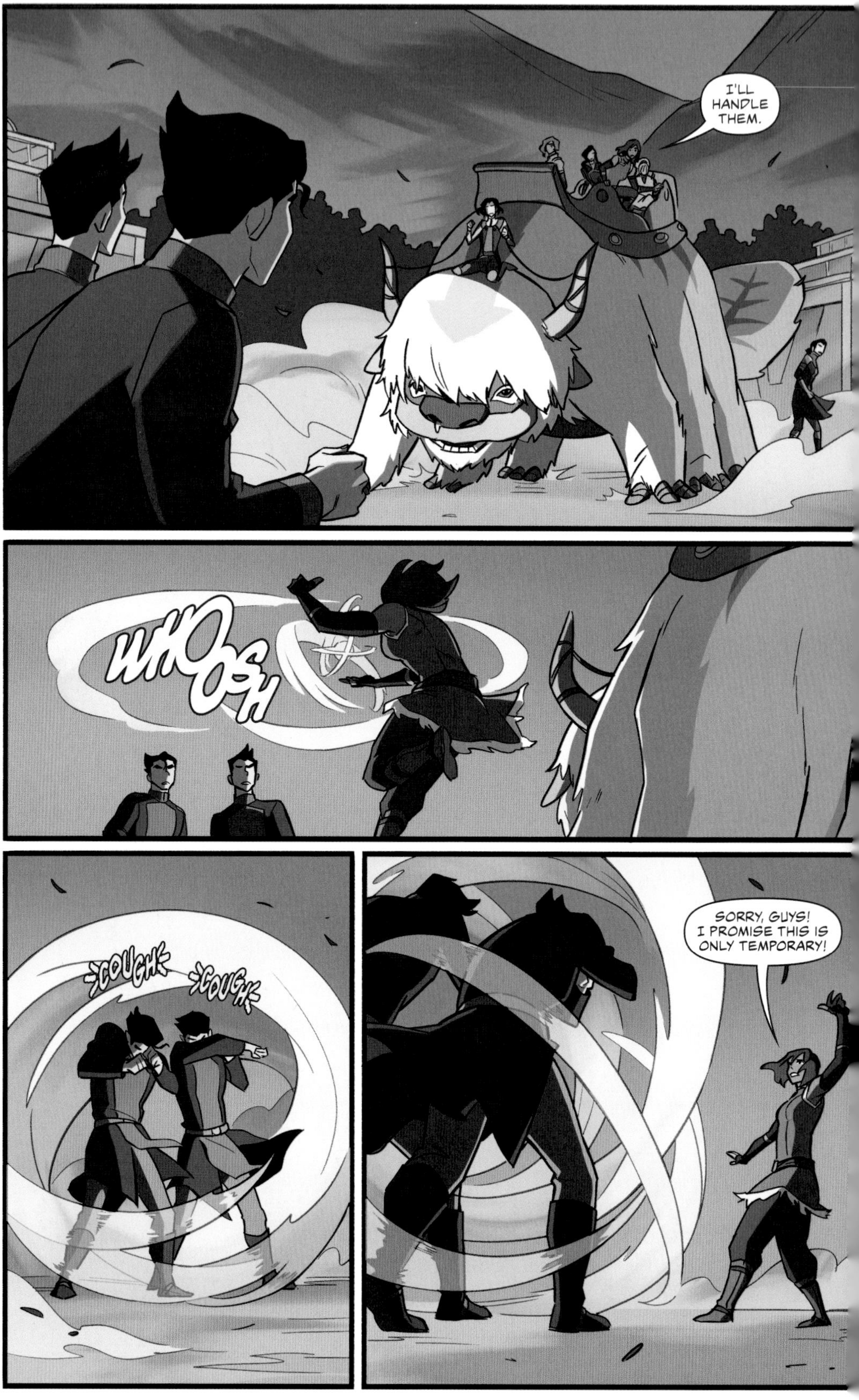
I'LL HANDLE THEM.
WHOOSH
COUGH
COUGH
SORRY, GUYS! I PROMISE THIS IS ONLY TEMPORARY!

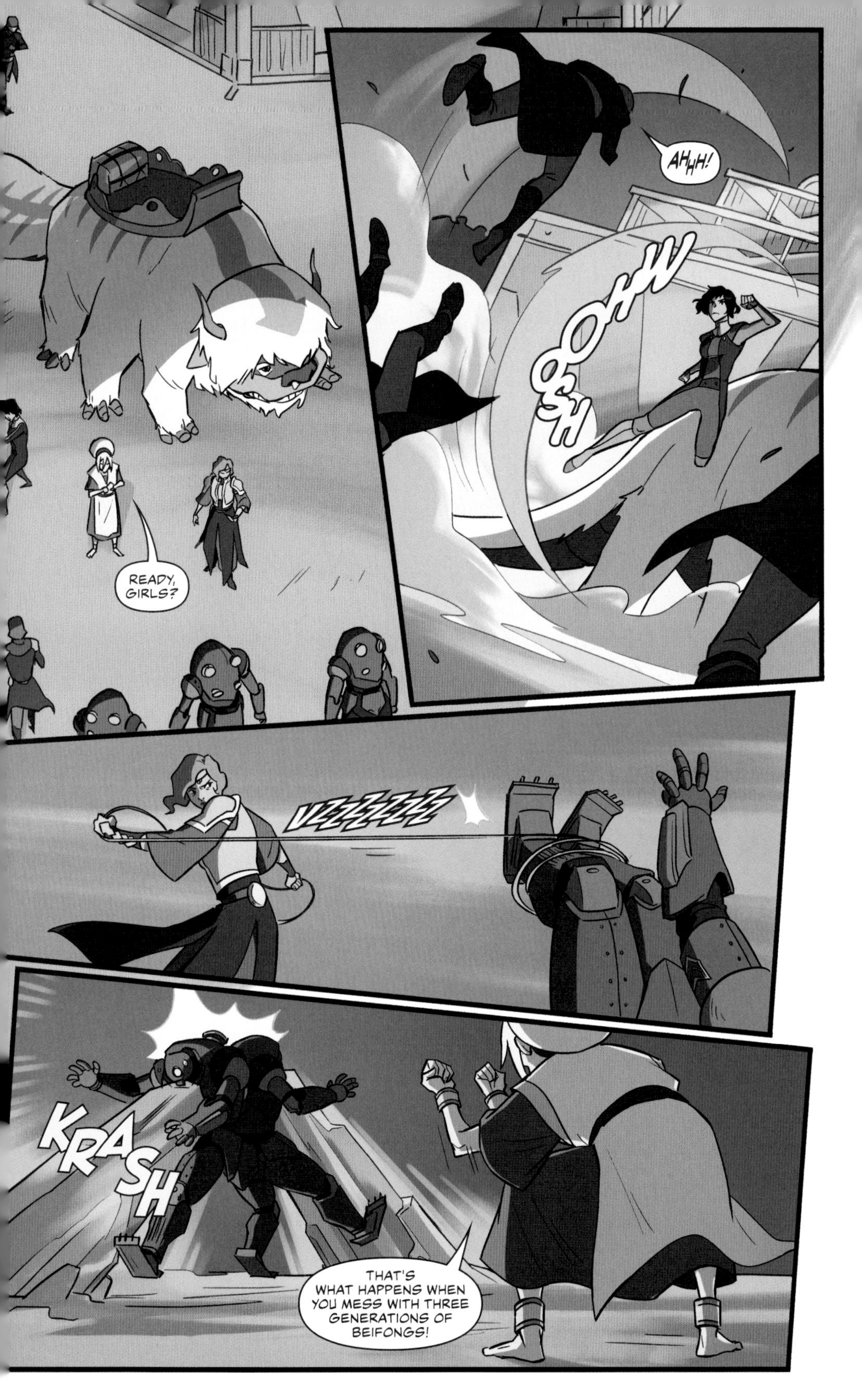
READY, GIRLS?
AHHH!
WHOOSH
VZZZZZZZ
KRASH
THAT'S WHAT HAPPENS WHEN YOU MESS WITH THREE GENERATIONS OF BEIFONGS!

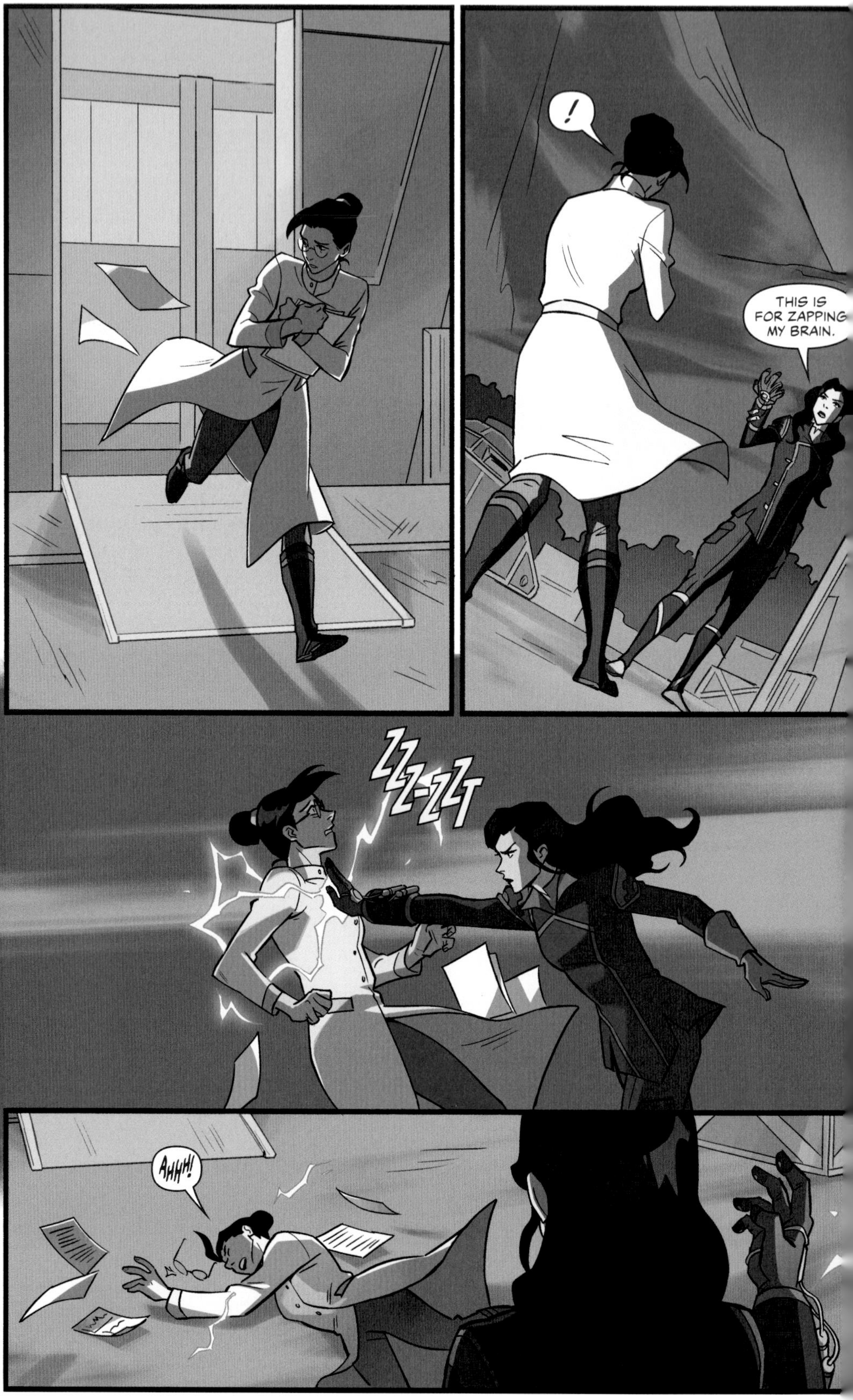
!
THIS IS FOR ZAPPING MY BRAIN.
ZZZ-ZZZT
AHHH!

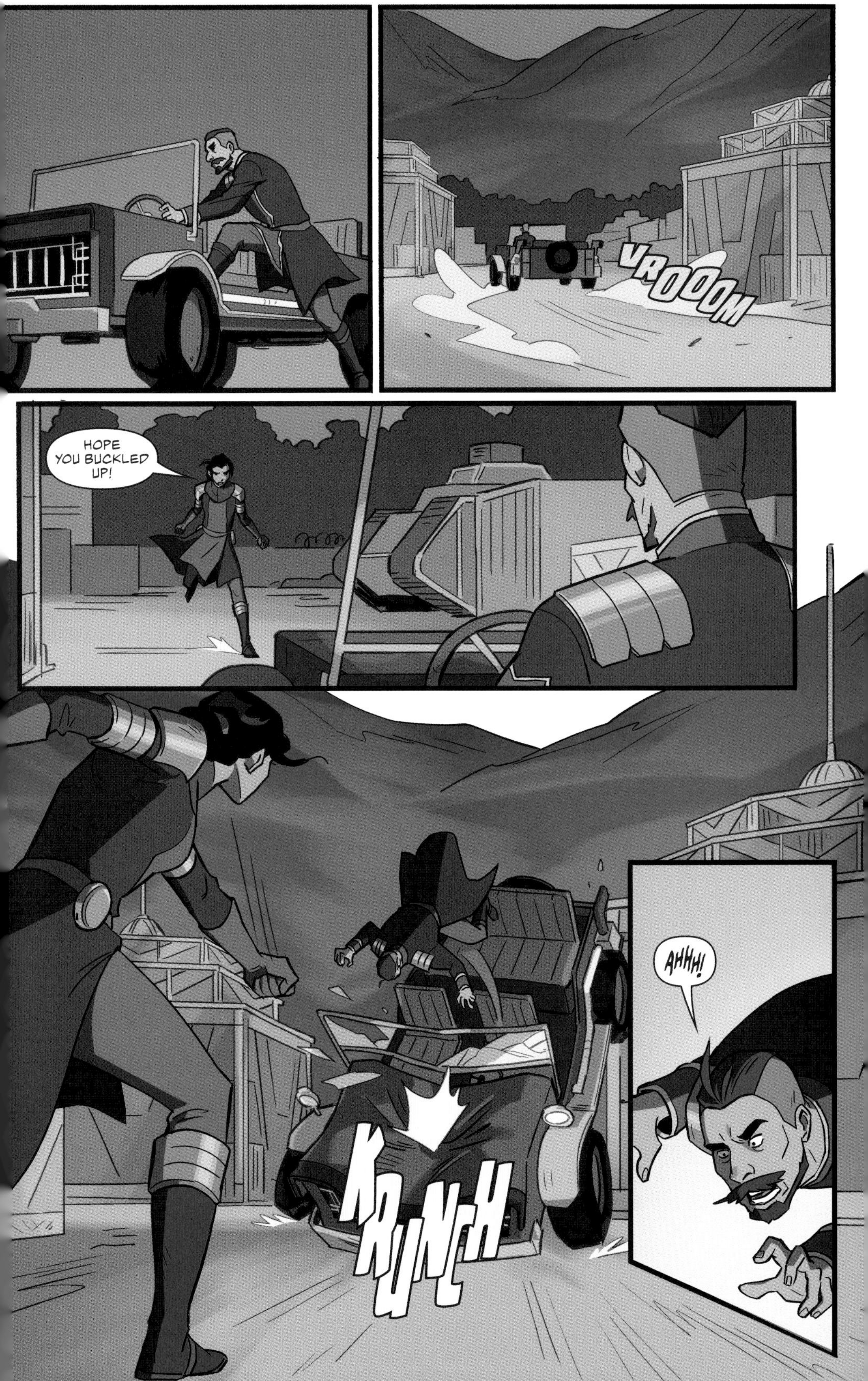
VROOOM
HOPE YOU BUCKLED UP!
AHHH!
KRUNCH

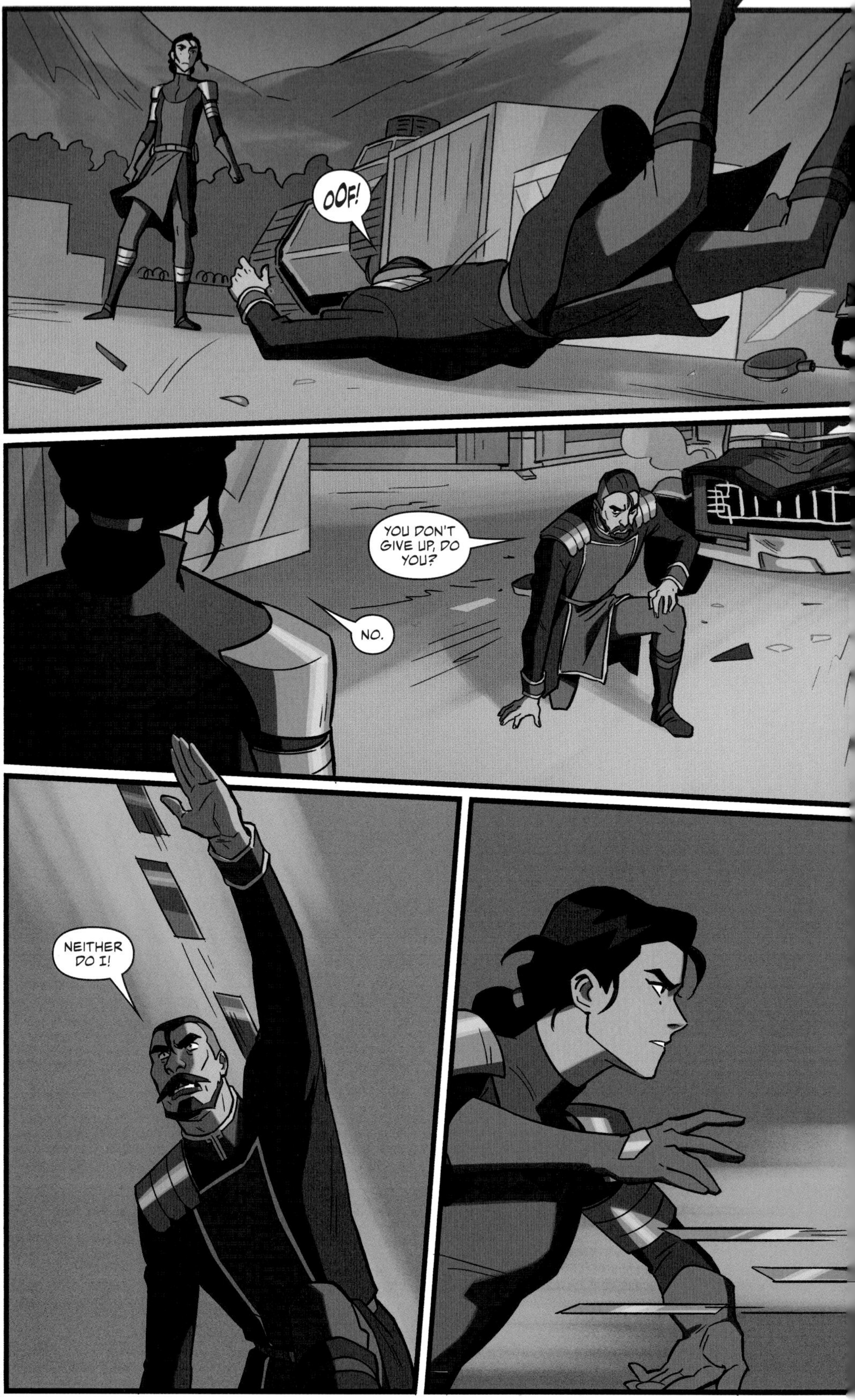
OOF!
YOU DON'T GIVE UP, DO YOU?
NO.
NEITHER DO I!

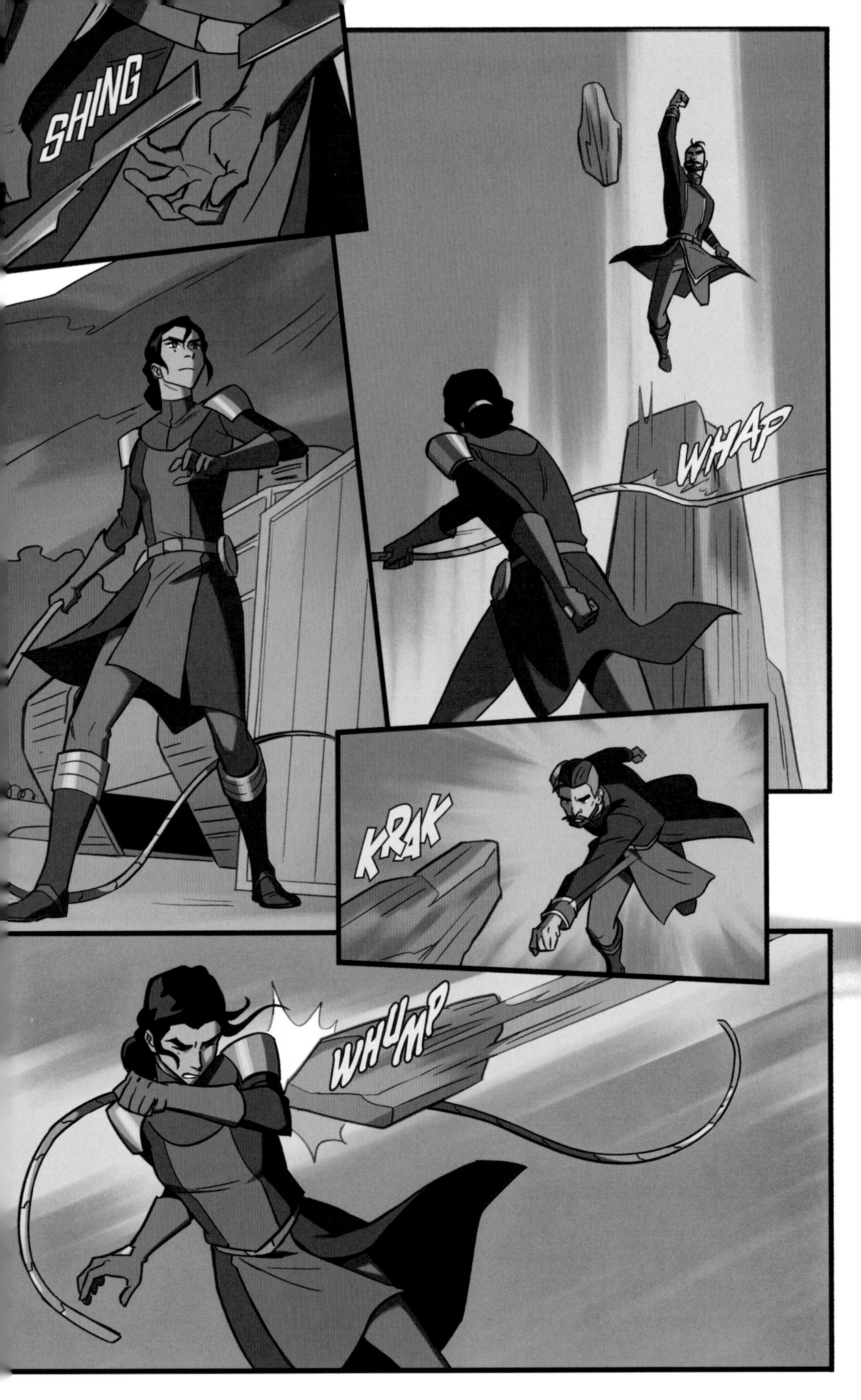
SHING
WHAP
KRAK
WHUMP

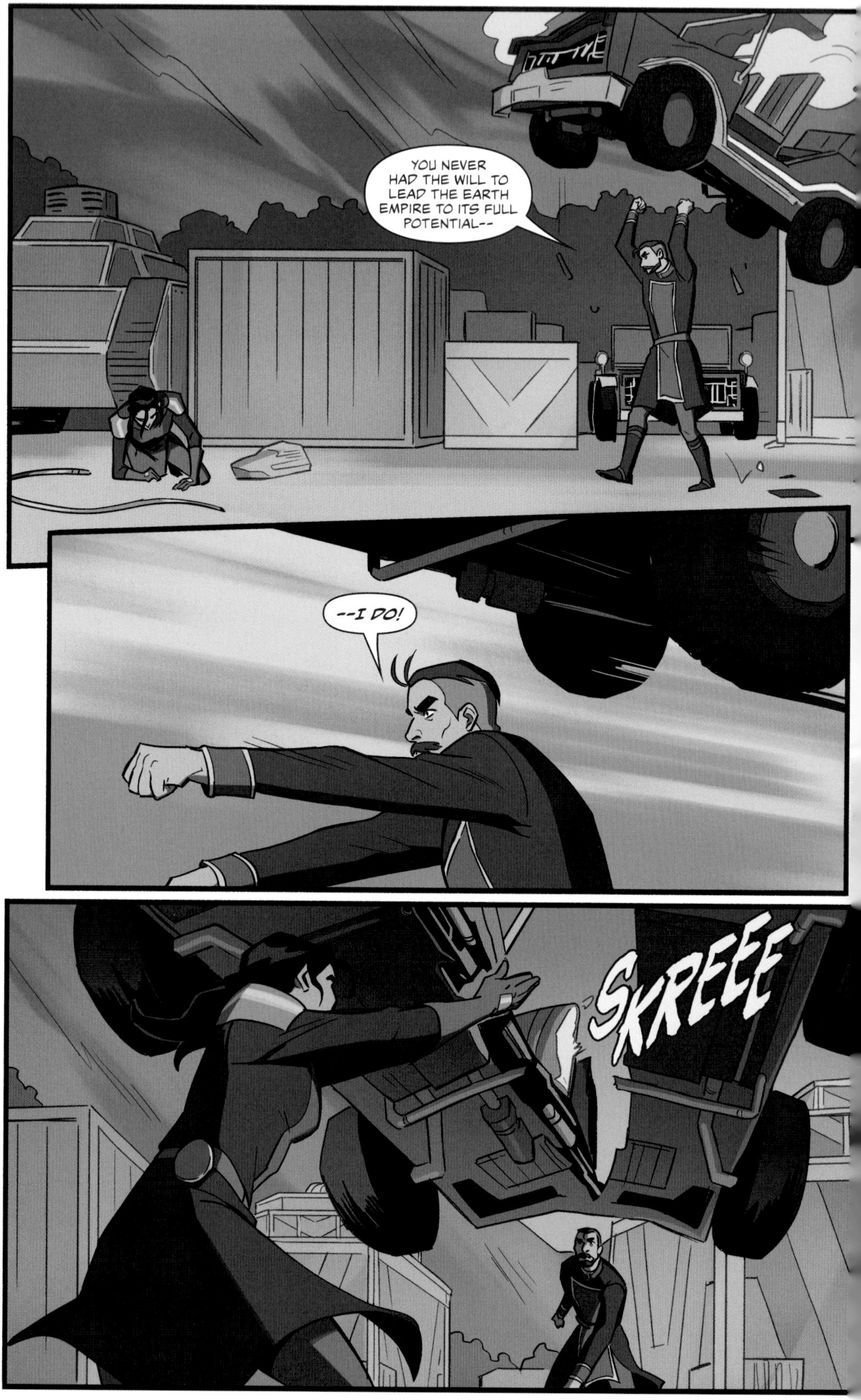
YOU NEVER HAD THE WILL TO LEAD THE EARTH EMPIRE TO ITS FULL POTENTIAL--
--I DO!
SKREEE

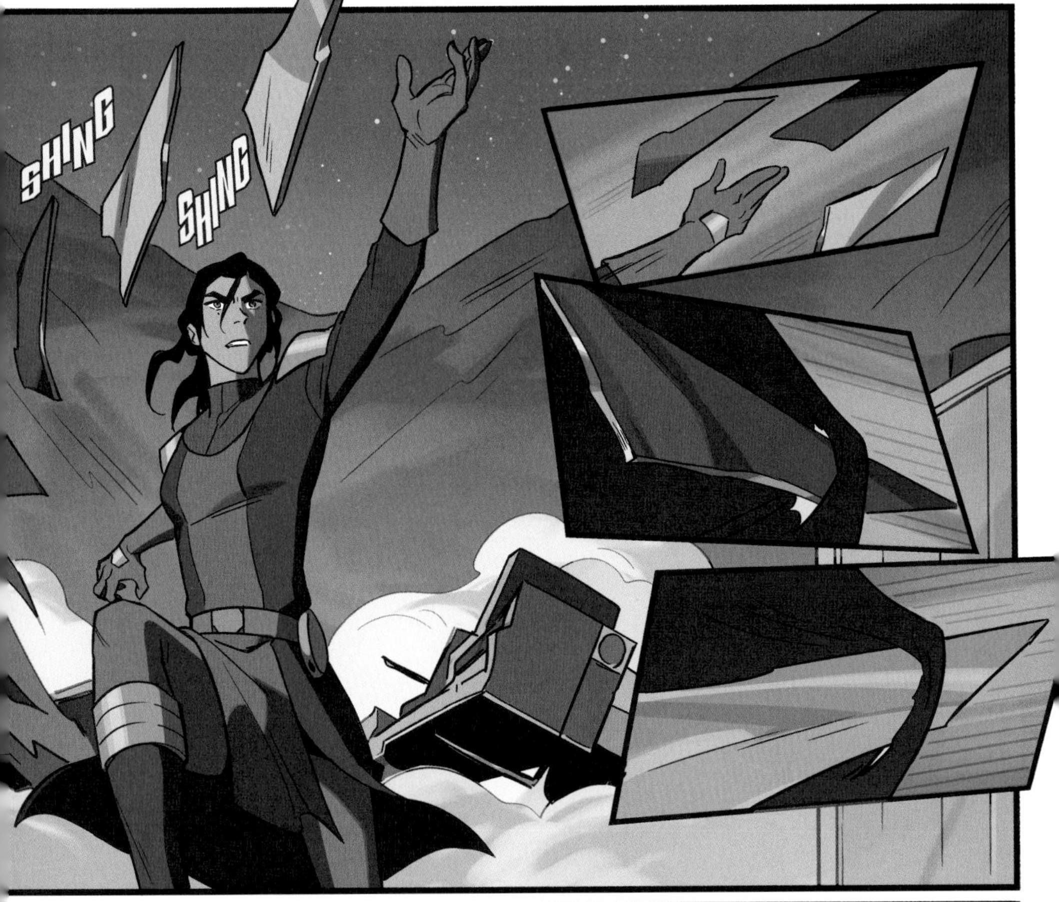
SHING
SHING

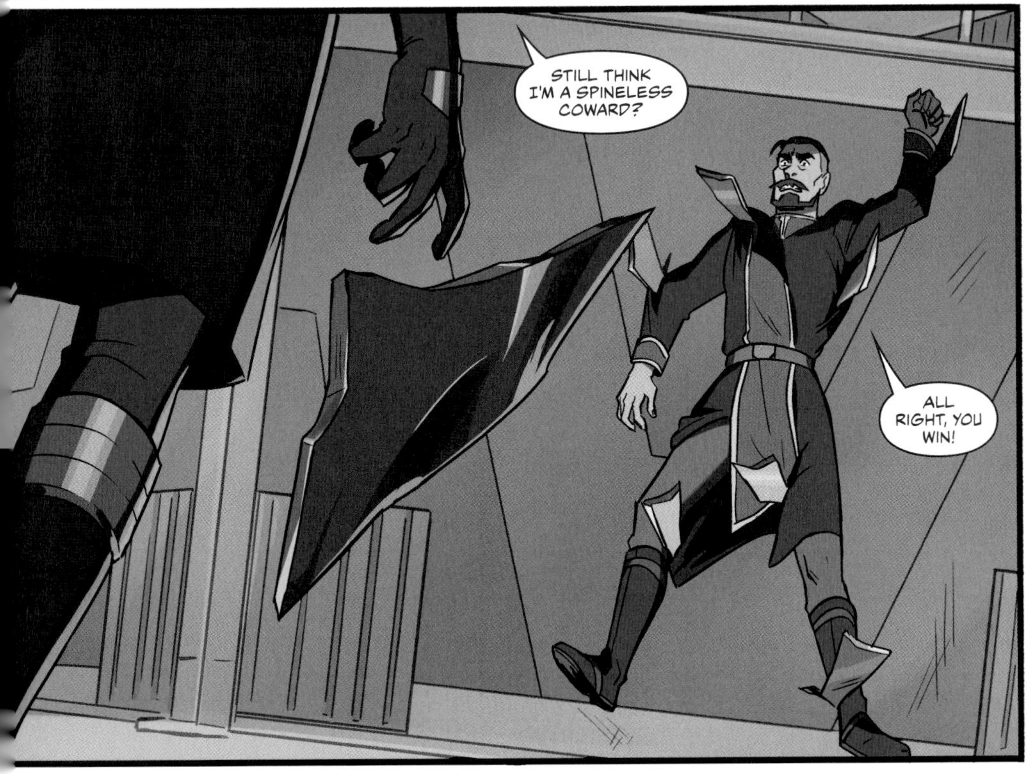
STILL THINK I'M A SPINELESS COWARD?
ALL RIGHT, YOU WIN!

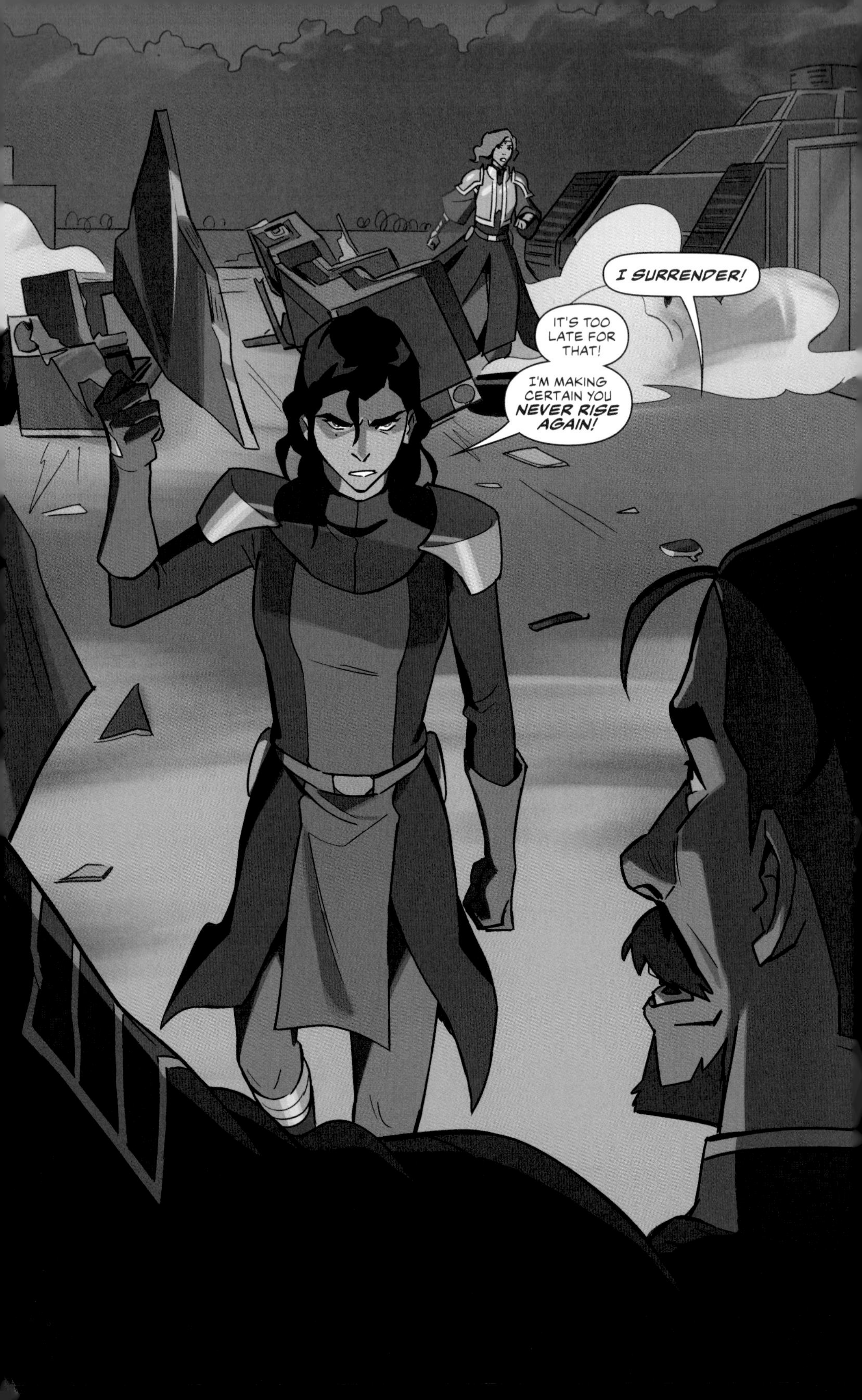
I SURRENDER!
IT'S TOO LATE FOR THAT!
I'M MAKING CERTAIN YOU NEVER RISE AGAIN!

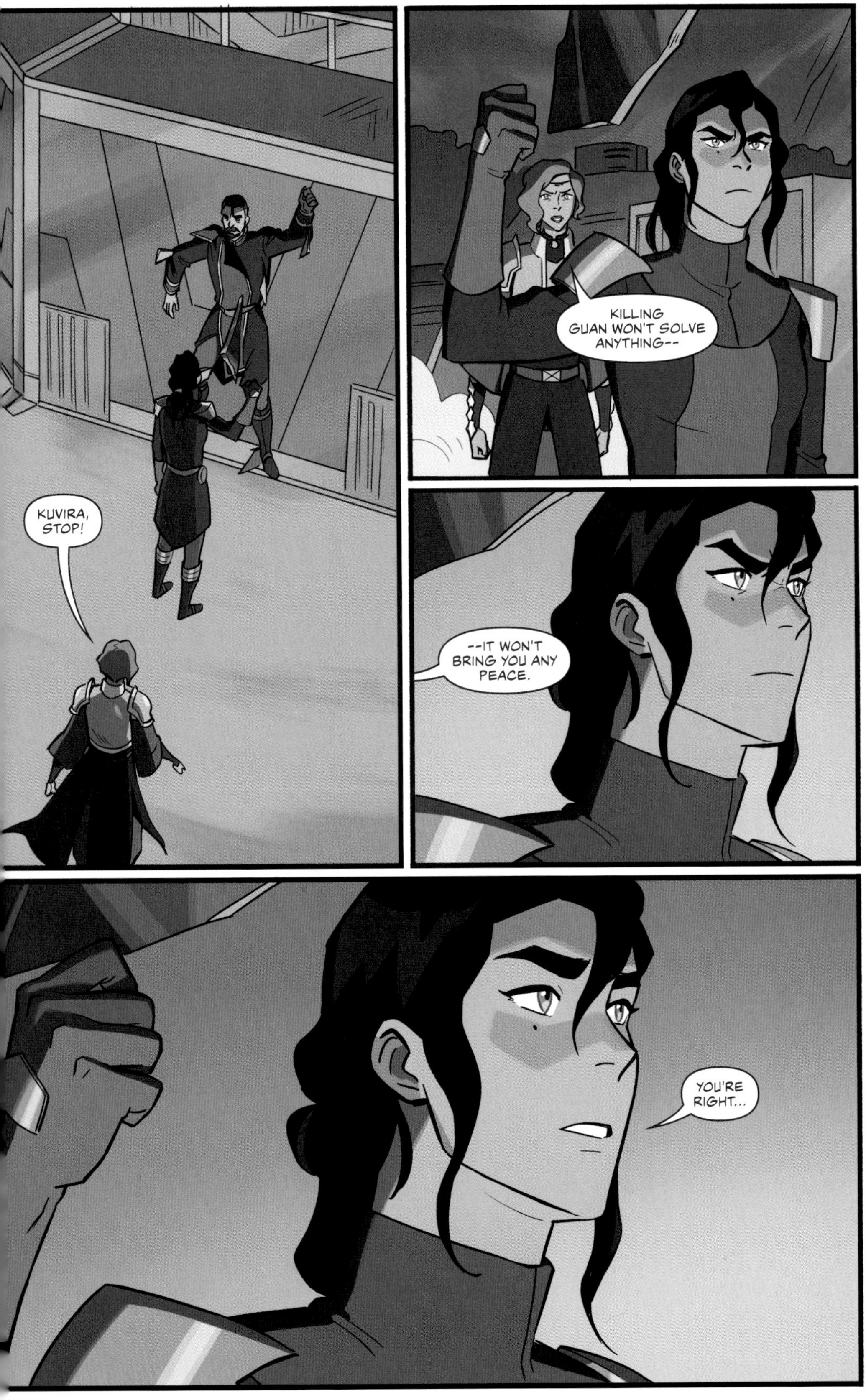
KUVIRA, STOP!
KILLING GUAN WON'T SOLVE ANYTHING--
--IT WON'T BRING YOU ANY PEACE.
YOU'RE RIGHT...

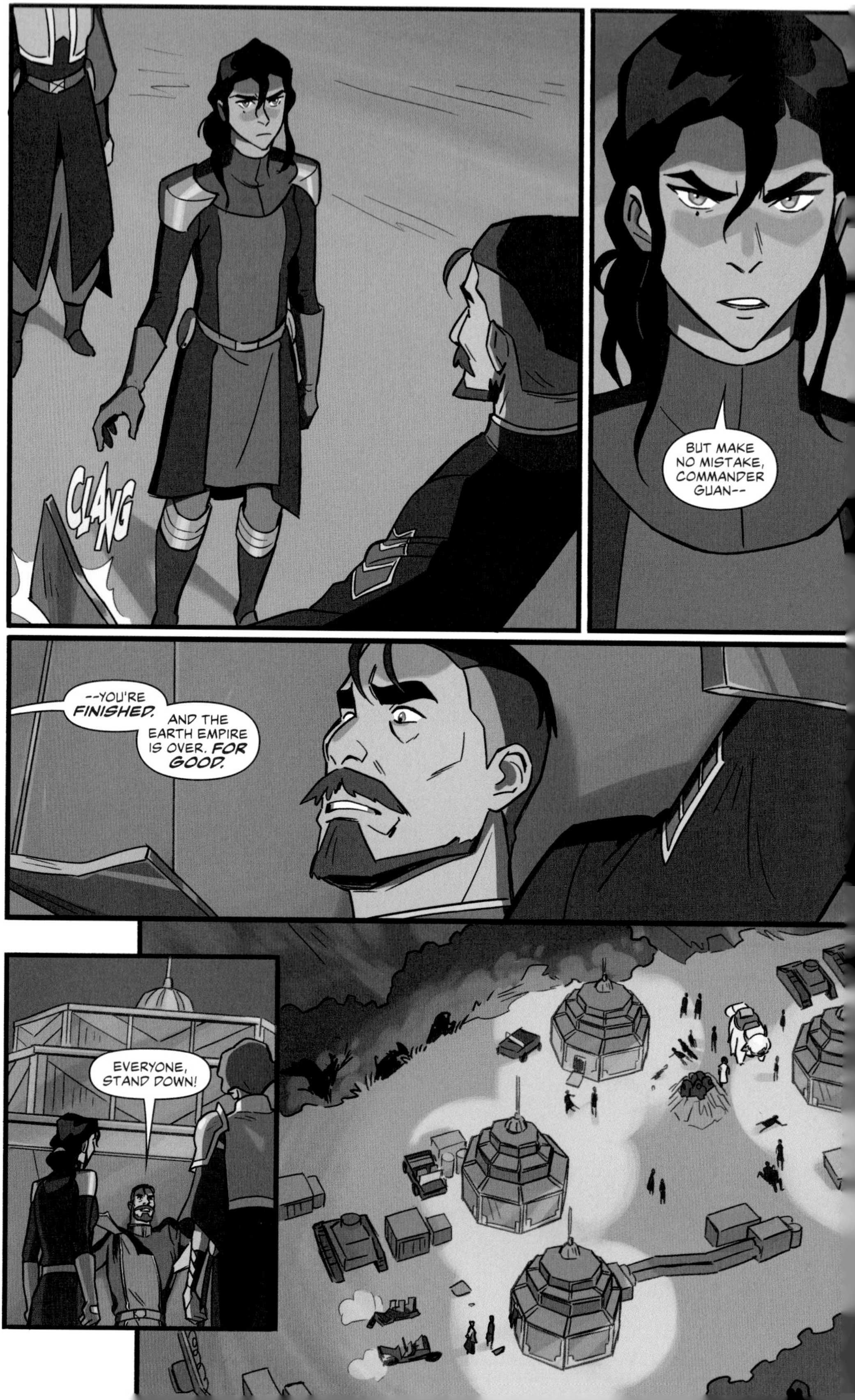
CLANG
BUT MAKE NO MISTAKE, COMMANDER GUAN--
--YOU'RE FINISHED. AND THE EARTH EMPIRE IS OVER. FOR GOOD.
EVERYONE, STAND DOWN!

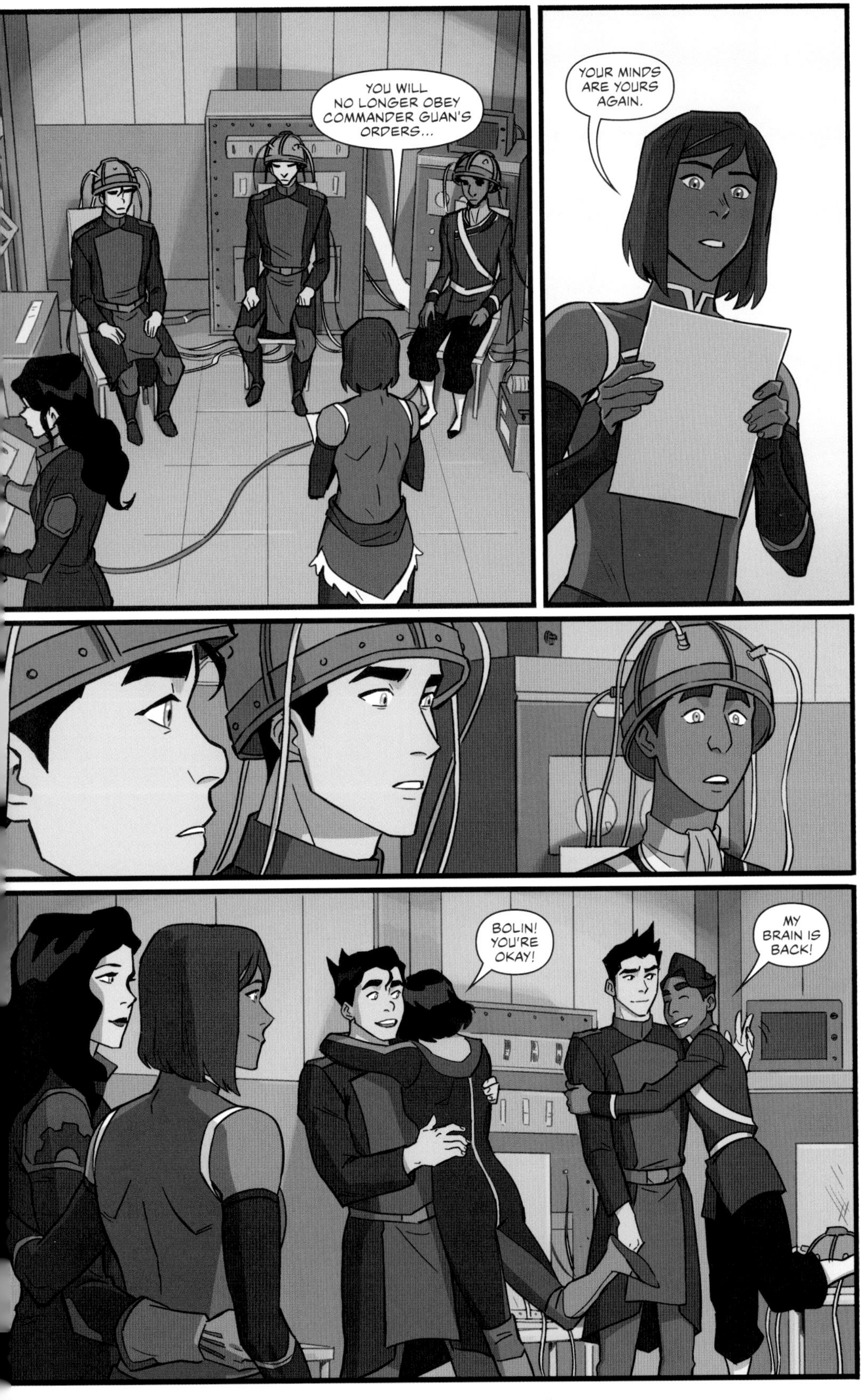
YOU WILL NO LONGER OBEY COMMANDER GUAN'S ORDERS...
YOUR MINDS ARE YOURS AGAIN.
BOLIN! YOU'RE OKAY!
MY BRAIN IS BACK!

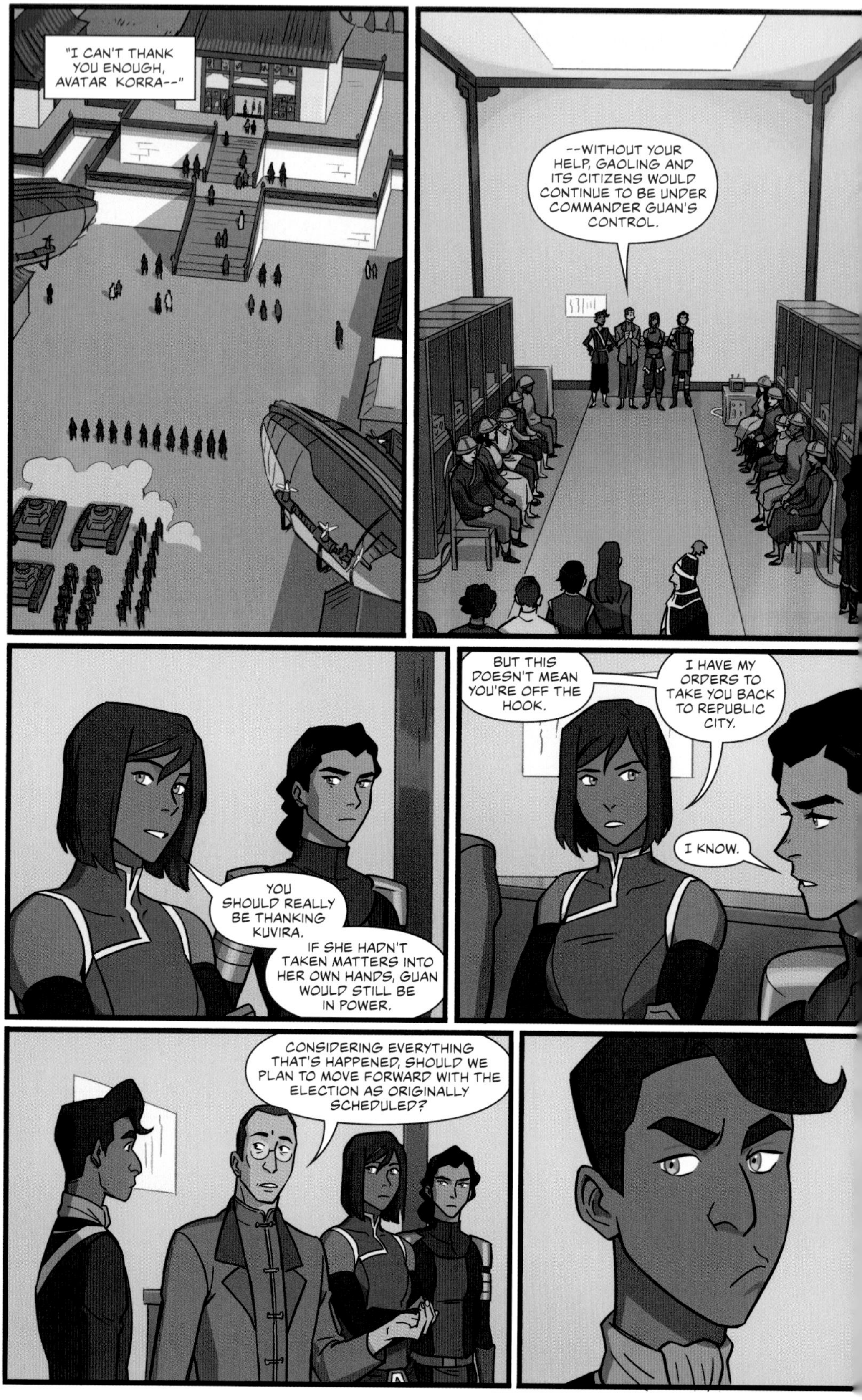
"I CAN'T THANK YOU ENOUGH, AVATAR KORRA--"
--WITHOUT YOUR HELP, GAOLING AND ITS CITIZENS WOULD CONTINUE TO BE UNDER COMMANDER GUAN'S CONTROL.
YOU SHOULD REALLY BE THANKING KUVIRA.
IF SHE HADN'T TAKEN MATTERS INTO HER OWN HANDS, GUAN WOULD STILL BE IN POWER.
BUT THIS DOESN'T MEAN YOU'RE OFF THE HOOK.
I HAVE MY ORDERS TO TAKE YOU BACK TO REPUBLIC CITY.
I KNOW.
CONSIDERING EVERYTHING THAT'S HAPPENED, SHOULD WE PLAN TO MOVE FORWARD WITH THE ELECTION AS ORIGINALLY SCHEDULED?

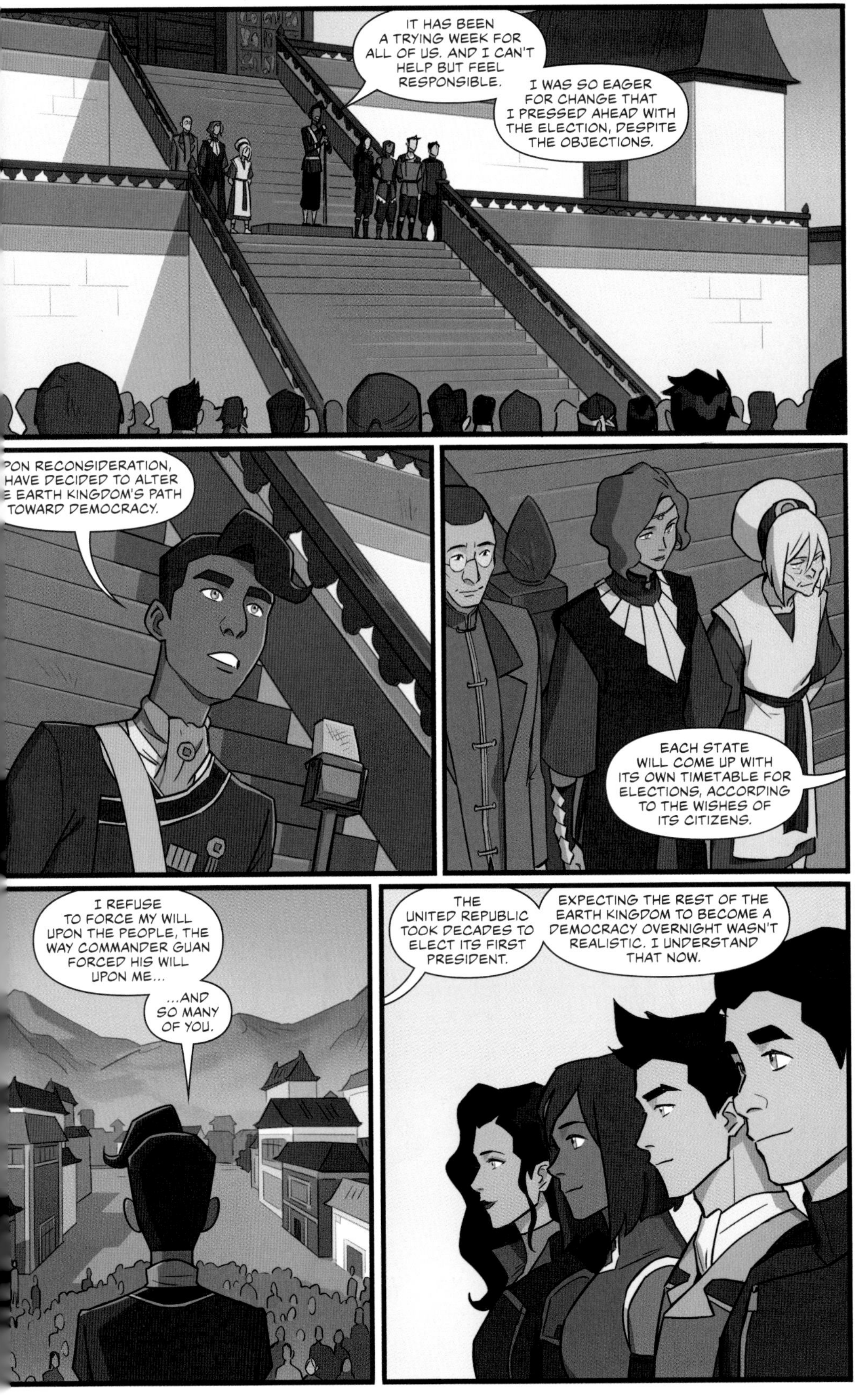
IT HAS BEEN A TRYING WEEK FOR ALL OF US. AND I CAN'T HELP BUT FEEL RESPONSIBLE.
I WAS SO EAGER FOR CHANGE THAT I PRESSED AHEAD WITH THE ELECTION, DESPITE THE OBJECTIONS.
PON RECONSIDERATION, HAVE DECIDED TO ALTER E EARTH KINGDOM'S PATH TOWARD DEMOCRACY.
EACH STATE WILL COME UP WITH ITS OWN TIMETABLE FOR ELECTIONS, ACCORDING TO THE WISHES OF ITS CITIZENS.
I REFUSE TO FORCE MY WILL UPON THE PEOPLE, THE WAY COMMANDER GUAN FORCED HIS WILL UPON ME...
...AND SO MANY OF YOU.
THE UNITED REPUBLIC TOOK DECADES TO ELECT ITS FIRST PRESIDENT.
EXPECTING THE REST OF THE EARTH KINGDOM TO BECOME A DEMOCRACY OVERNIGHT WASN'T REALISTIC. I UNDERSTAND THAT NOW.

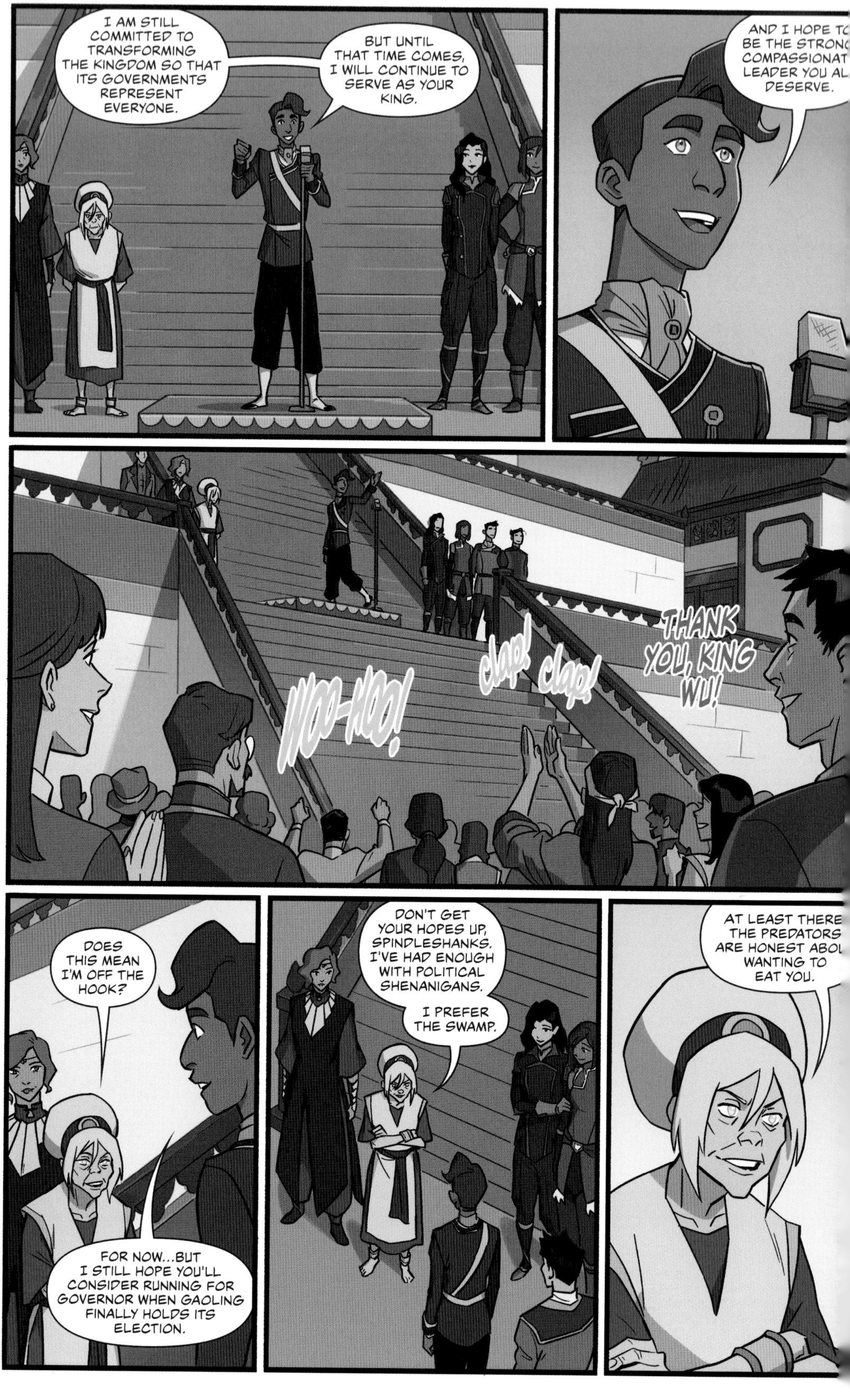
I AM STILL COMMITTED TO TRANSFORMING THE KINGDOM SO THAT ITS GOVERNMENTS REPRESENT EVERYONE.
BUT UNTIL THAT TIME COMES, I WILL CONTINUE TO SERVE AS YOUR KING.
AND I HOPE T BE THE STRON COMPASSIONAT LEADER YOU AL DESERVE.
WOO-HOO!
clap! clap!
THANK YOU, KING WU!
DOES THIS MEAN I'M OFF THE HOOK?
FOR NOW...BUT I STILL HOPE YOU'LL CONSIDER RUNNING FOR GOVERNOR WHEN GAOLING FINALLY HOLDS ITS ELECTION.
DON'T GET YOUR HOPES UP, SPINDLESHANKS. I'VE HAD ENOUGH WITH POLITICAL SHENANIGANS.
I PREFER THE SWAMP.
AT LEAST THERE THE PREDATORS ARE HONEST ABO WANTING TO EAT YOU.

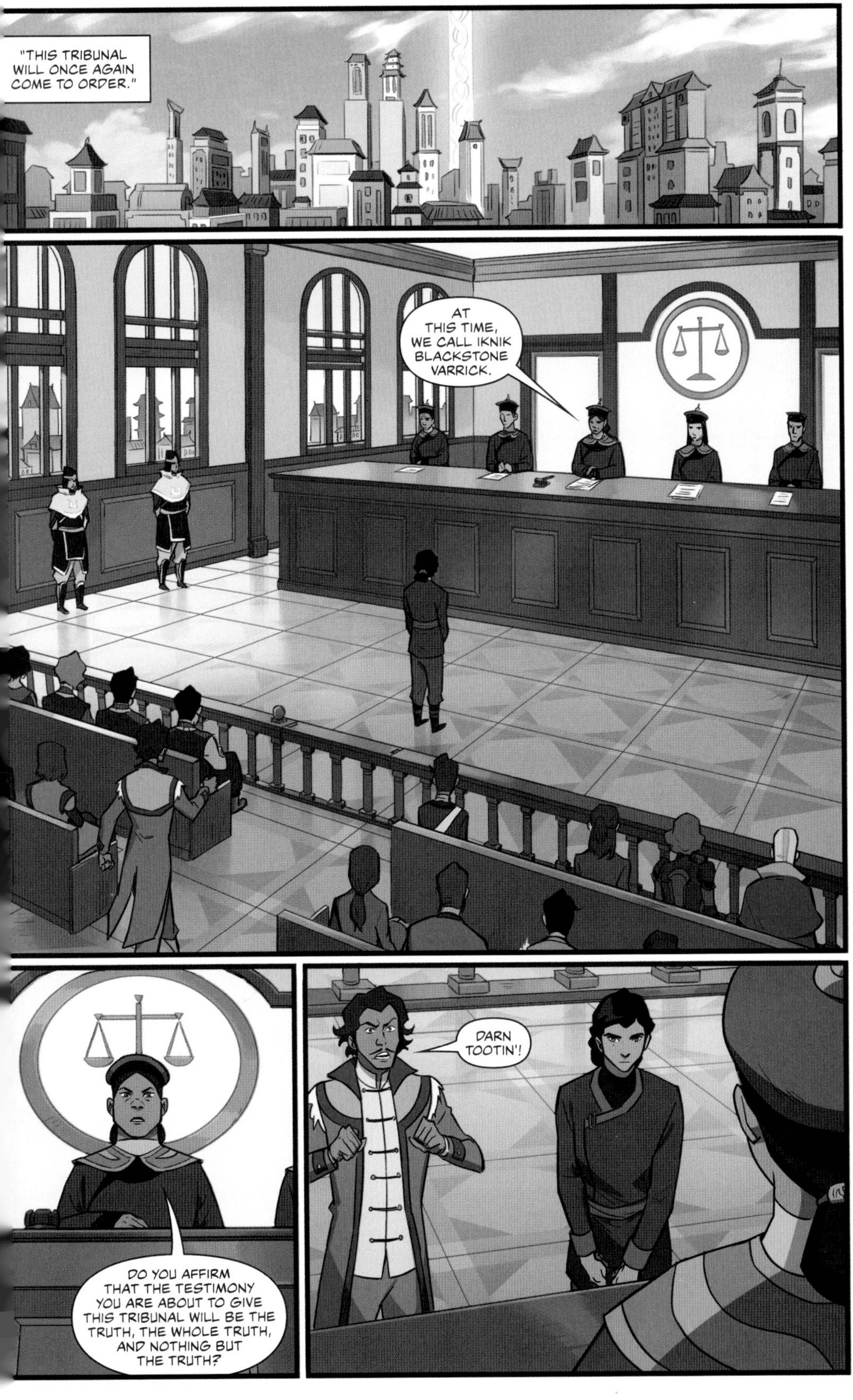
"THIS TRIBUNAL WILL ONCE AGAIN COME TO ORDER."
AT THIS TIME, WE CALL IKNIK BLACKSTONE VARRICK.
DO YOU AFFIRM THAT THE TESTIMONY YOU ARE ABOUT TO GIVE THIS TRIBUNAL WILL BE THE TRUTH, THE WHOLE TRUTH, AND NOTHING BUT THE TRUTH?
DARN TOOTIN'!

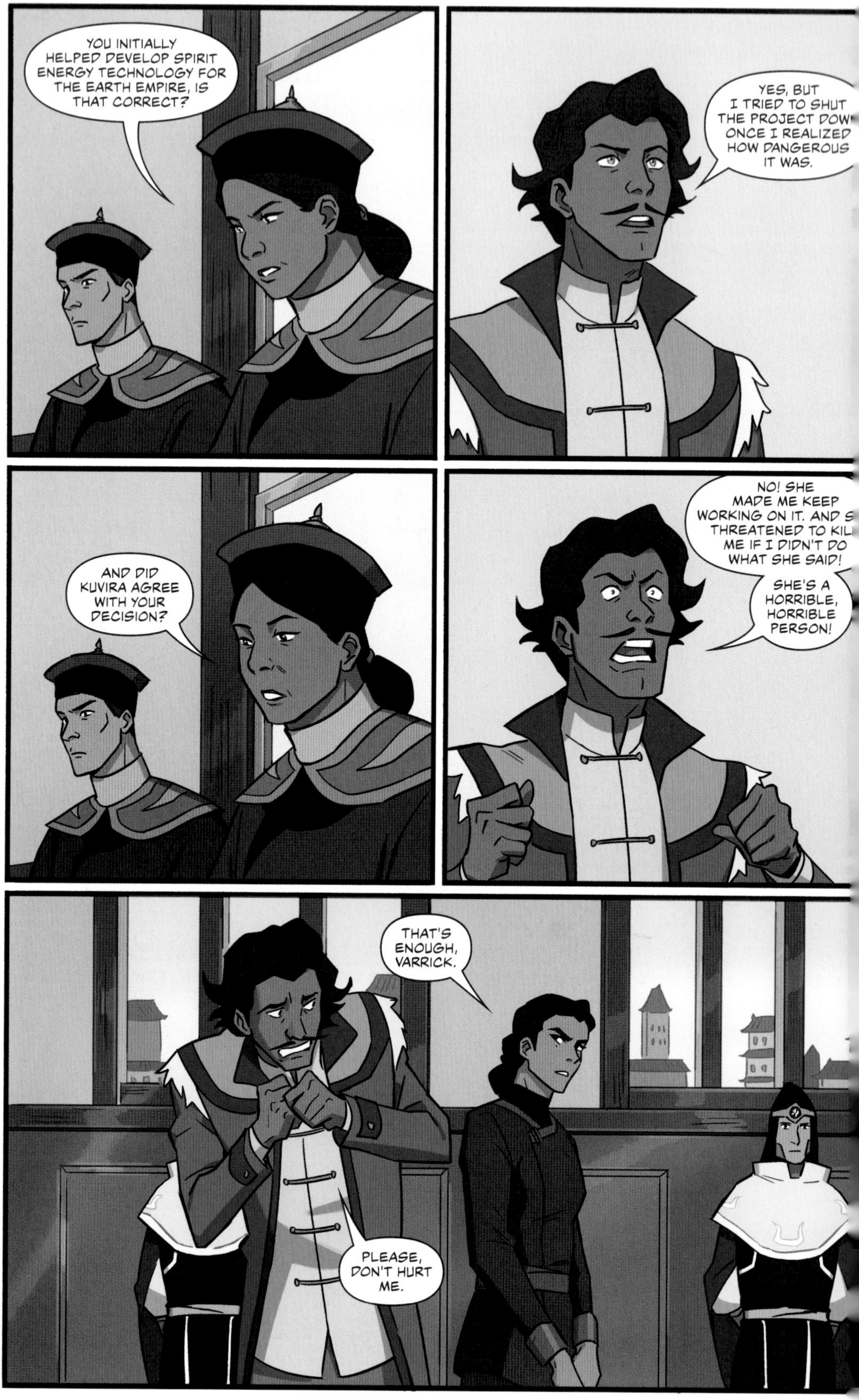
YOU INITIALLY HELPED DEVELOP SPIRIT ENERGY TECHNOLOGY FOR THE EARTH EMPIRE, IS THAT CORRECT?
YES, BUT I TRIED TO SHUT THE PROJECT DOW ONCE I REALIZED HOW DANGEROUS IT WAS.
AND DID KUVIRA AGREE WITH YOUR DECISION?
NO! SHE MADE ME KEEP WORKING ON IT. AND S THREATENED TO KIL ME IF I DIDN'T DO WHAT SHE SAID!
SHE'S A HORRIBLE, HORRIBLE PERSON!
THAT'S ENOUGH, VARRICK.
PLEASE, DON'T HURT ME.

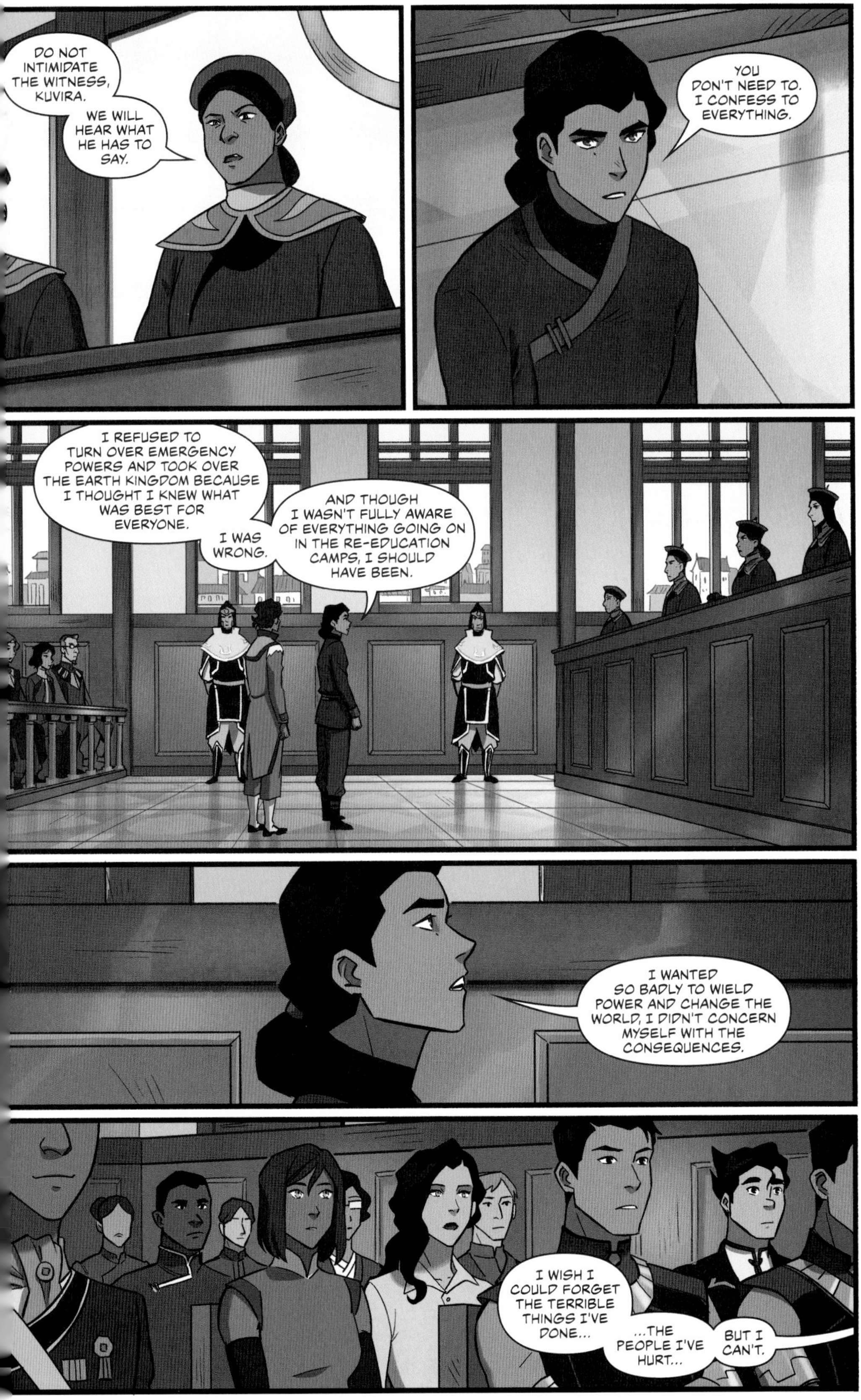
DO NOT INTIMIDATE THE WITNESS, KUVIRA.
WE WILL HEAR WHAT HE HAS TO SAY.
YOU DON'T NEED TO. I CONFESS TO EVERYTHING.
I REFUSED TO TURN OVER EMERGENCY POWERS AND TOOK OVER THE EARTH KINGDOM BECAUSE I THOUGHT I KNEW WHAT WAS BEST FOR EVERYONE.
I WAS WRONG.
AND THOUGH I WASN'T FULLY AWARE OF EVERYTHING GOING ON IN THE RE-EDUCATION CAMPS, I SHOULD HAVE BEEN.
I WANTED SO BADLY TO WIELD POWER AND CHANGE THE WORLD, I DIDN'T CONCERN MYSELF WITH THE CONSEQUENCES.
I WISH I COULD FORGET THE TERRIBLE THINGS I'VE DONE...
...THE PEOPLE I'VE HURT...
BUT I CAN'T.

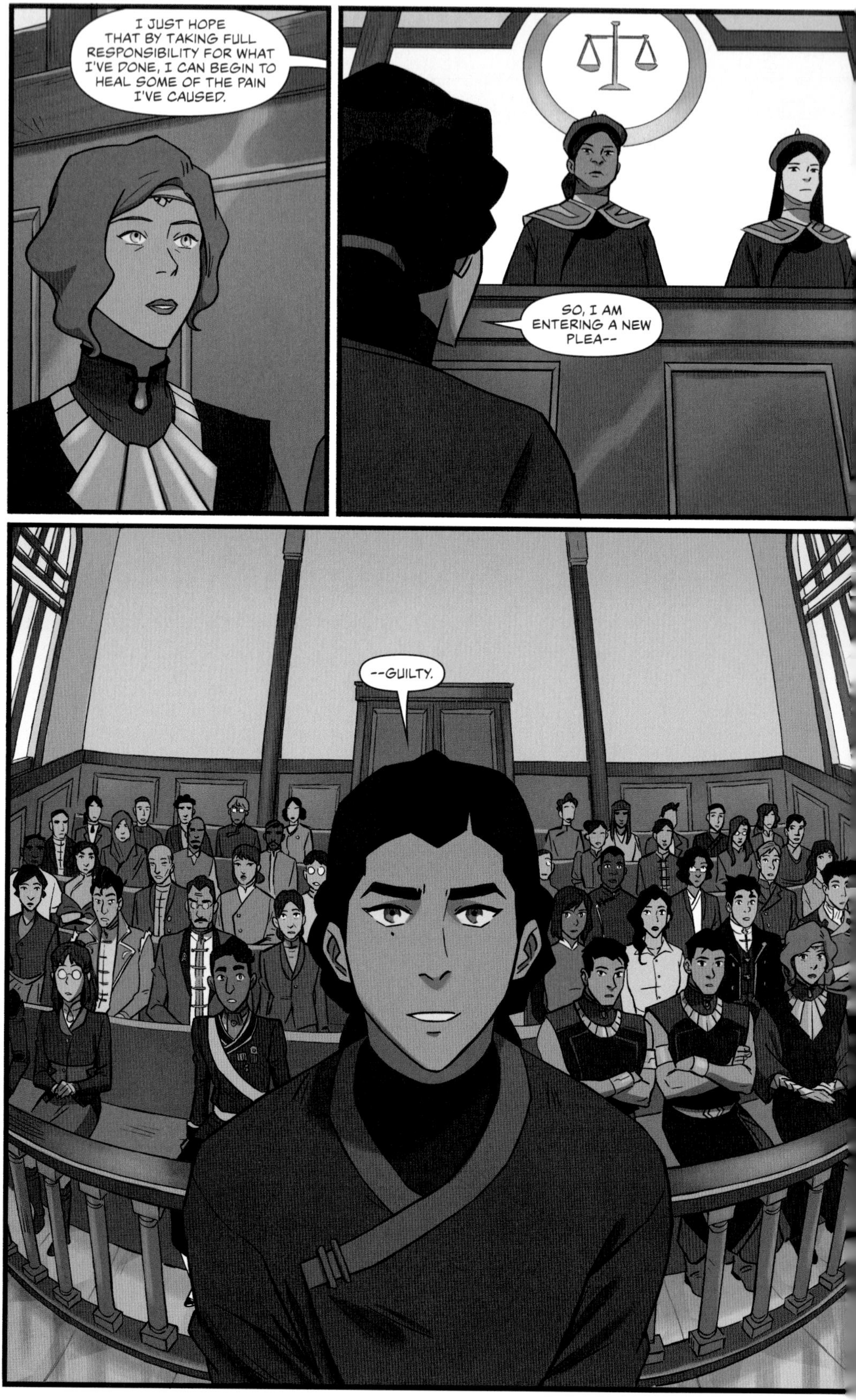
I JUST HOPE THAT BY TAKING FULL RESPONSIBILITY FOR WHAT I'VE DONE, I CAN BEGIN TO HEAL SOME OF THE PAIN I'VE CAUSED.
SO, I AM ENTERING A NEW PLEA--
--GUILTY.

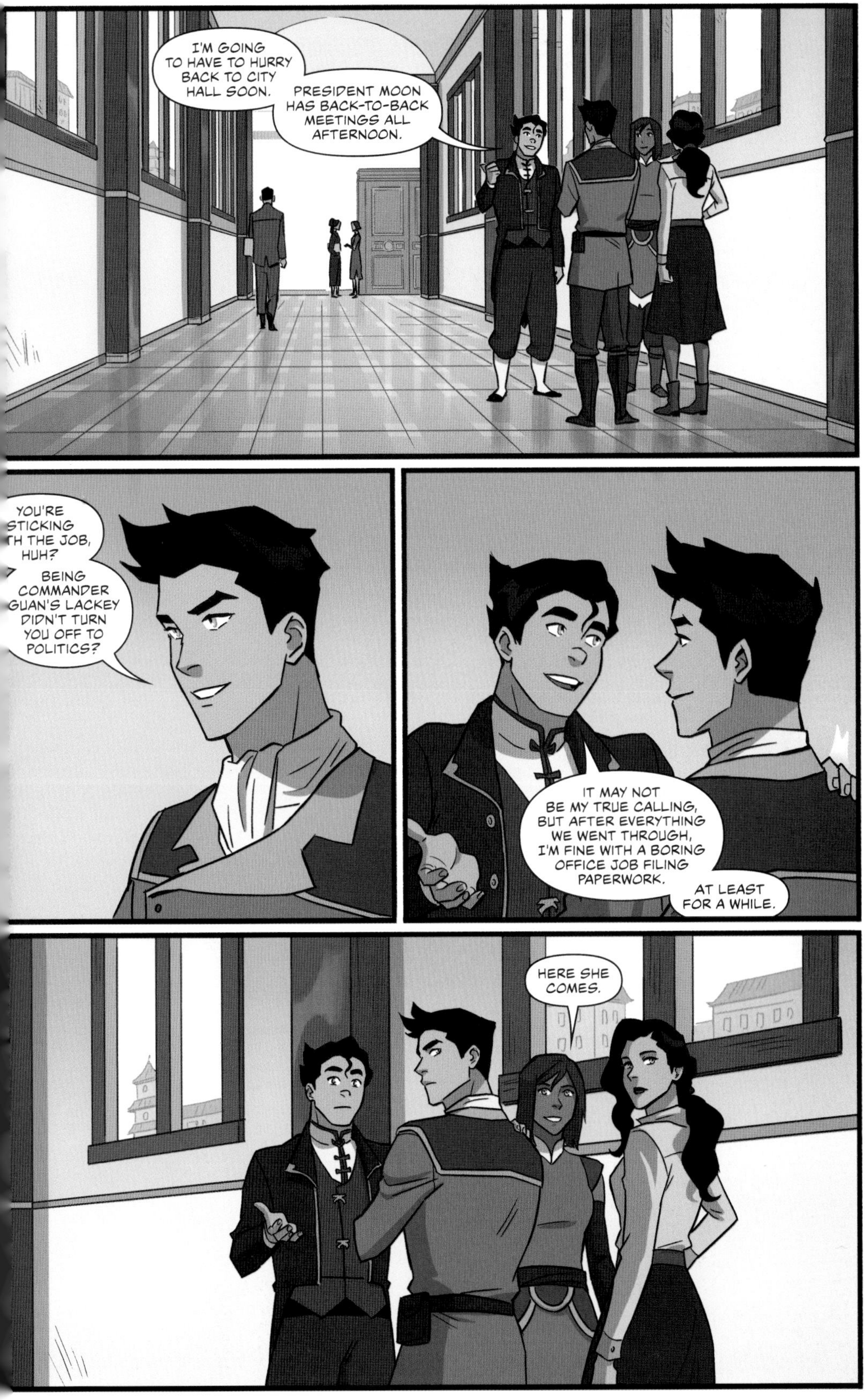
I'M GOING TO HAVE TO HURRY BACK TO CITY HALL SOON.
PRESIDENT MOON HAS BACK-TO-BACK MEETINGS ALL AFTERNOON.
YOU'RE STICKING TH THE JOB, HUH?
BEING COMMANDER GUAN'S LACKEY DIDN'T TURN YOU OFF TO POLITICS?
IT MAY NOT BE MY TRUE CALLING, BUT AFTER EVERYTHING WE WENT THROUGH, I'M FINE WITH A BORING OFFICE JOB FILING PAPERWORK.
AT LEAST FOR A WHILE.
HERE SHE COMES.

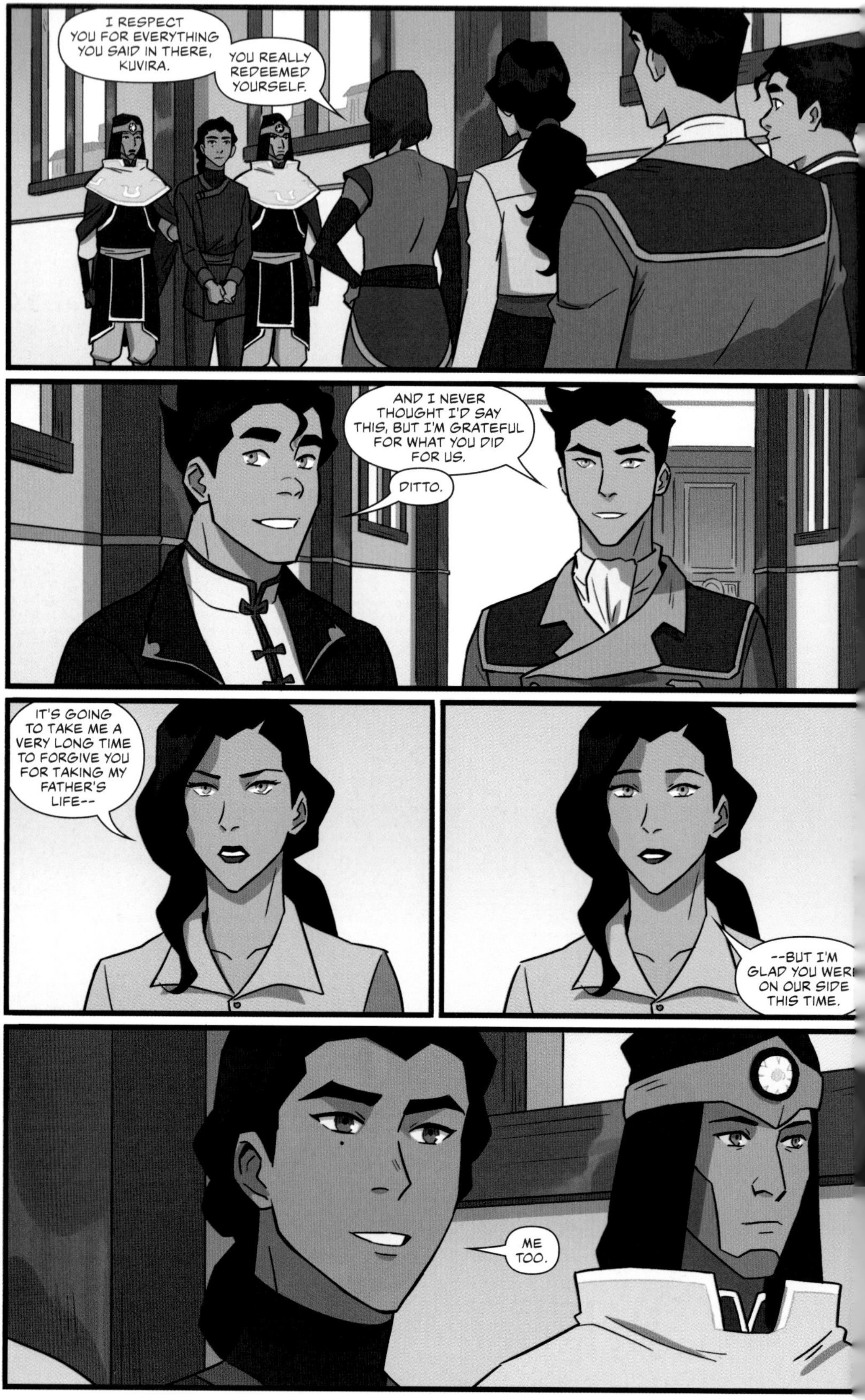
I RESPECT YOU FOR EVERYTHING YOU SAID IN THERE, KUVIRA.
YOU REALLY REDEEMED YOURSELF.
AND I NEVER THOUGHT I'D SAY THIS, BUT I'M GRATEFUL FOR WHAT YOU DID FOR US.
DITTO.
IT'S GOING TO TAKE ME A VERY LONG TIME TO FORGIVE YOU FOR TAKING MY FATHER'S LIFE--
--BUT I'M GLAD YOU WERE ON OUR SIDE THIS TIME.
ME TOO.

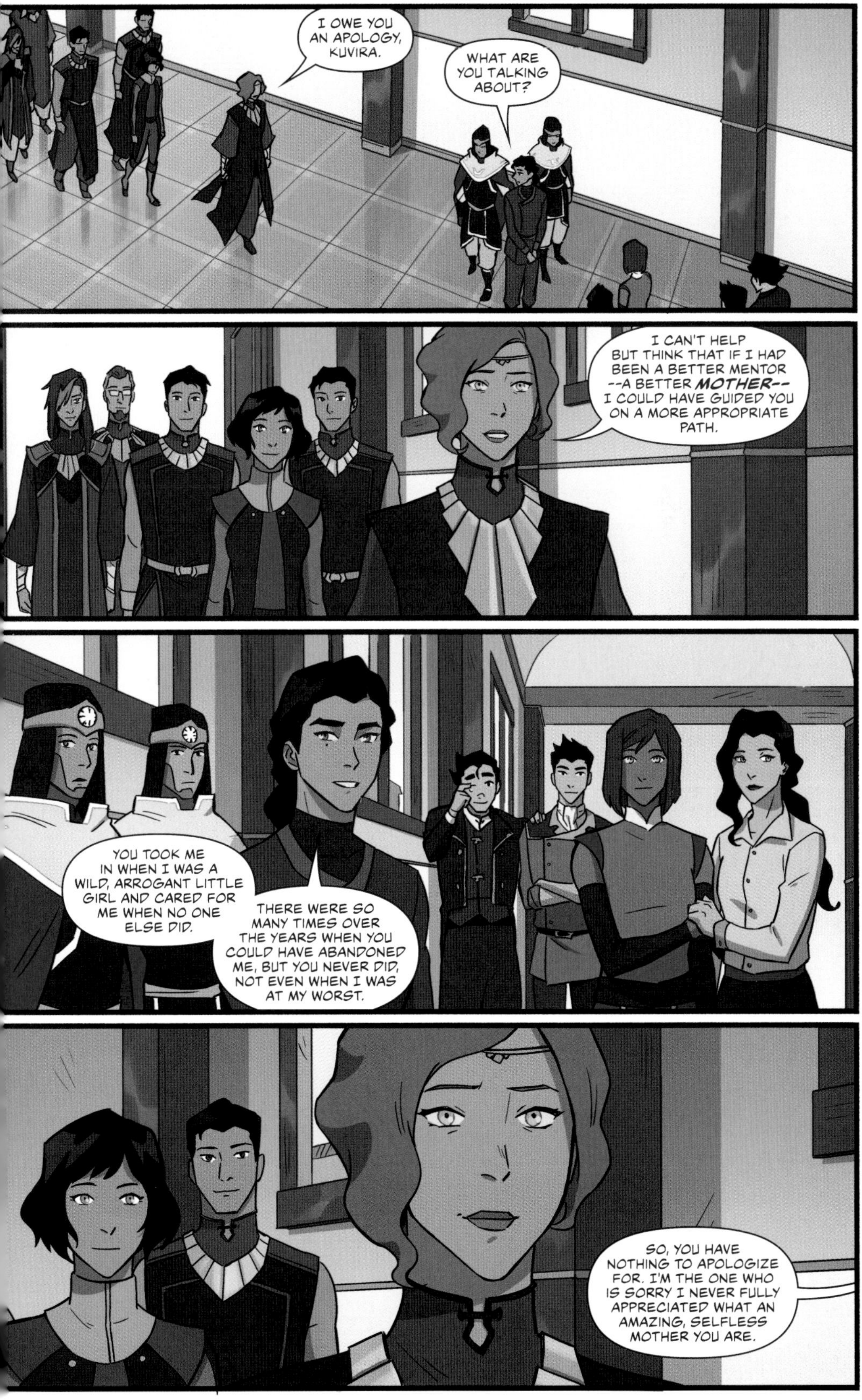
I OWE YOU AN APOLOGY, KUVIRA.
WHAT ARE YOU TALKING ABOUT?
I CAN'T HELP BUT THINK THAT IF I HAD BEEN A BETTER MENTOR --A BETTER *MOTHER*-- I COULD HAVE GUIDED YOU ON A MORE APPROPRIATE PATH.
YOU TOOK ME IN WHEN I WAS A WILD, ARROGANT LITTLE GIRL AND CARED FOR ME WHEN NO ONE ELSE DID.
THERE WERE SO MANY TIMES OVER THE YEARS WHEN YOU COULD HAVE ABANDONED ME, BUT YOU NEVER DID, NOT EVEN WHEN I WAS AT MY WORST.
SO, YOU HAVE NOTHING TO APOLOGIZE FOR. I'M THE ONE WHO IS SORRY I NEVER FULLY APPRECIATED WHAT AN AMAZING, SELFLESS MOTHER YOU ARE.

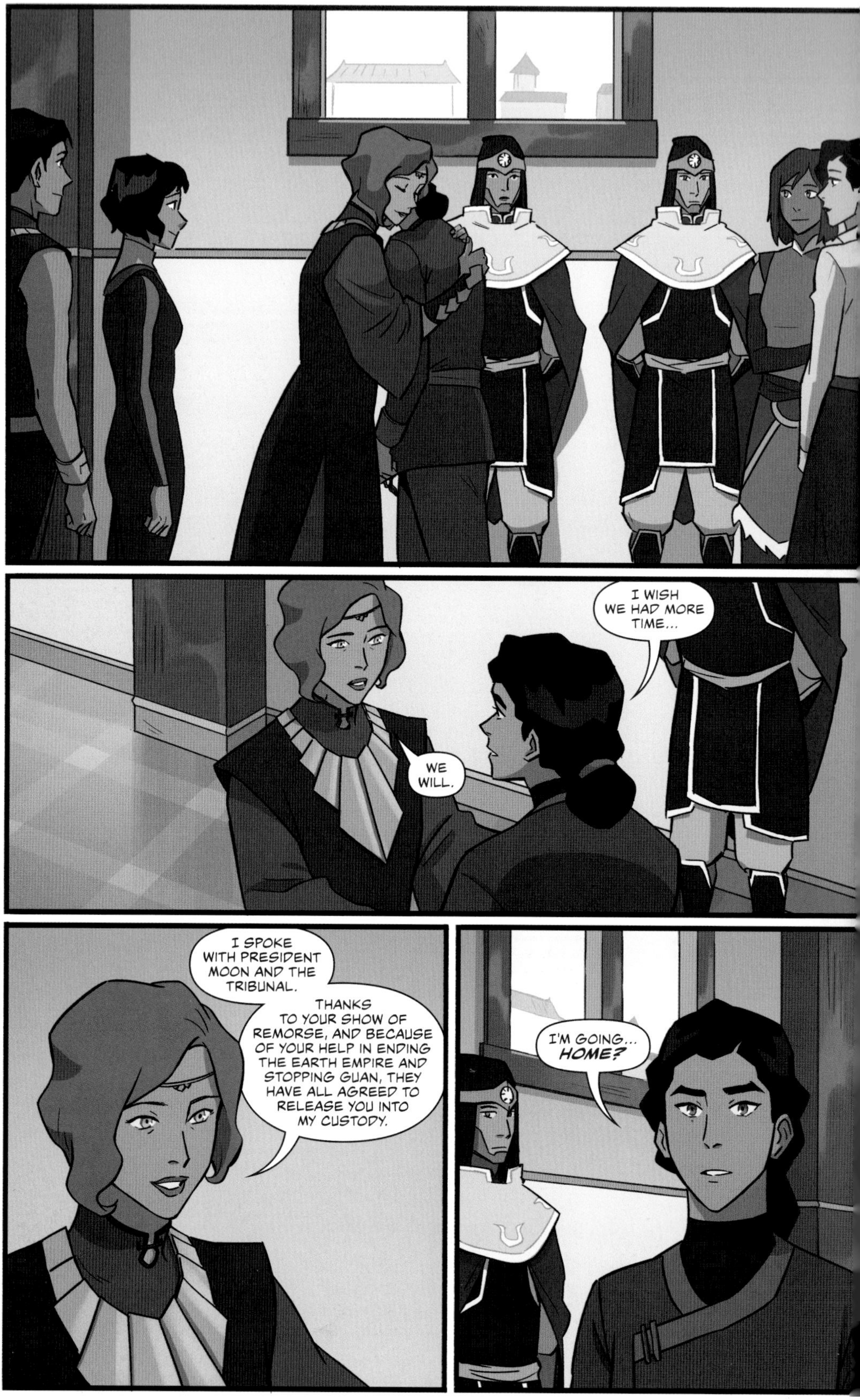
I WISH WE HAD MORE TIME...
WE WILL.
I SPOKE WITH PRESIDENT MOON AND THE TRIBUNAL.
THANKS TO YOUR SHOW OF REMORSE, AND BECAUSE OF YOUR HELP IN ENDING THE EARTH EMPIRE AND STOPPING GUAN, THEY HAVE ALL AGREED TO RELEASE YOU INTO MY CUSTODY.
I'M GOING... *HOME?*

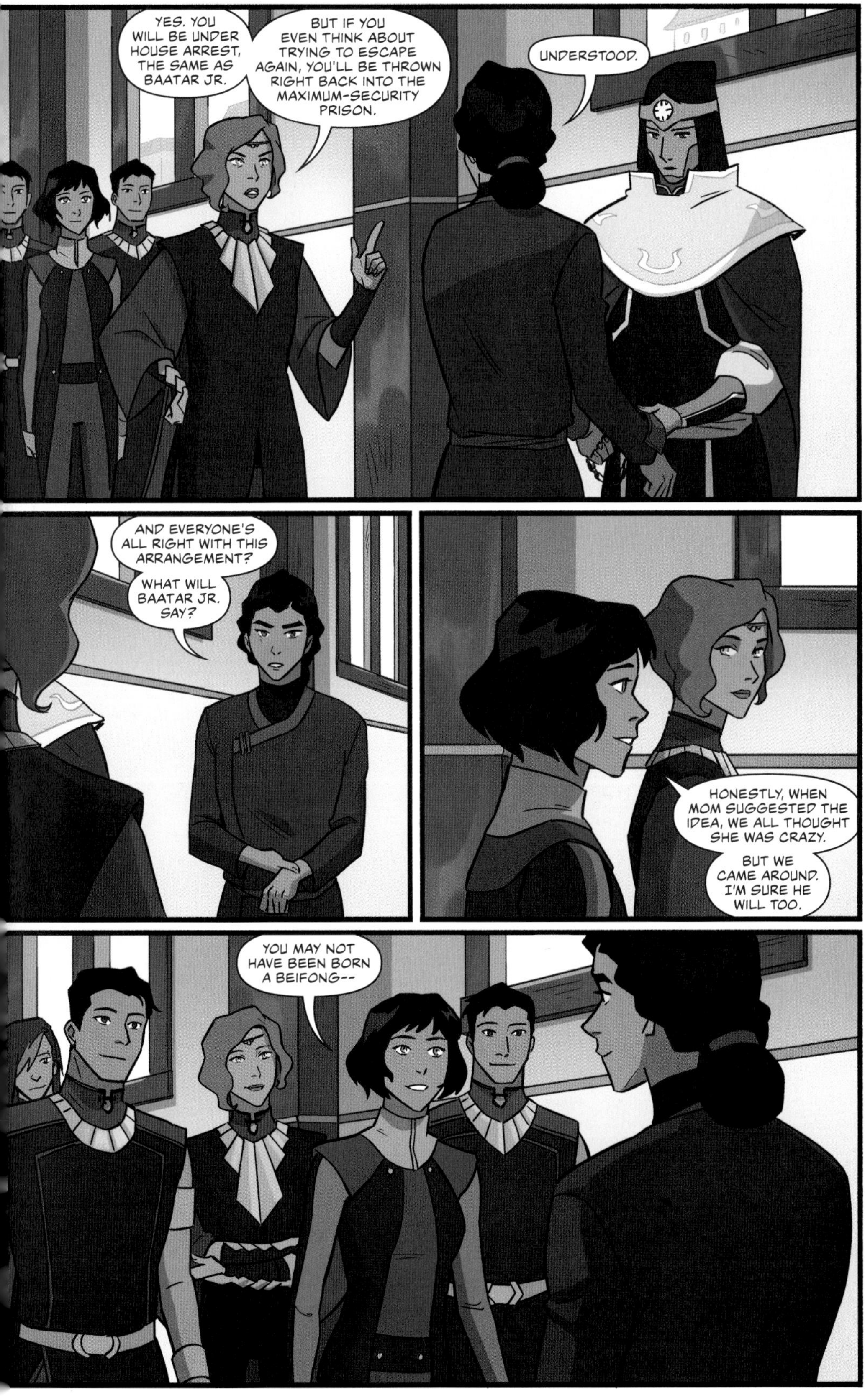
YES. YOU WILL BE UNDER HOUSE ARREST, THE SAME AS BAATAR JR.
BUT IF YOU EVEN THINK ABOUT TRYING TO ESCAPE AGAIN, YOU'LL BE THROWN RIGHT BACK INTO THE MAXIMUM-SECURITY PRISON.
UNDERSTOOD.
AND EVERYONE'S ALL RIGHT WITH THIS ARRANGEMENT?
WHAT WILL BAATAR JR. SAY?
HONESTLY, WHEN MOM SUGGESTED THE IDEA, WE ALL THOUGHT SHE WAS CRAZY.
BUT WE CAME AROUND. I'M SURE HE WILL TOO.
YOU MAY NOT HAVE BEEN BORN A BEIFONG--

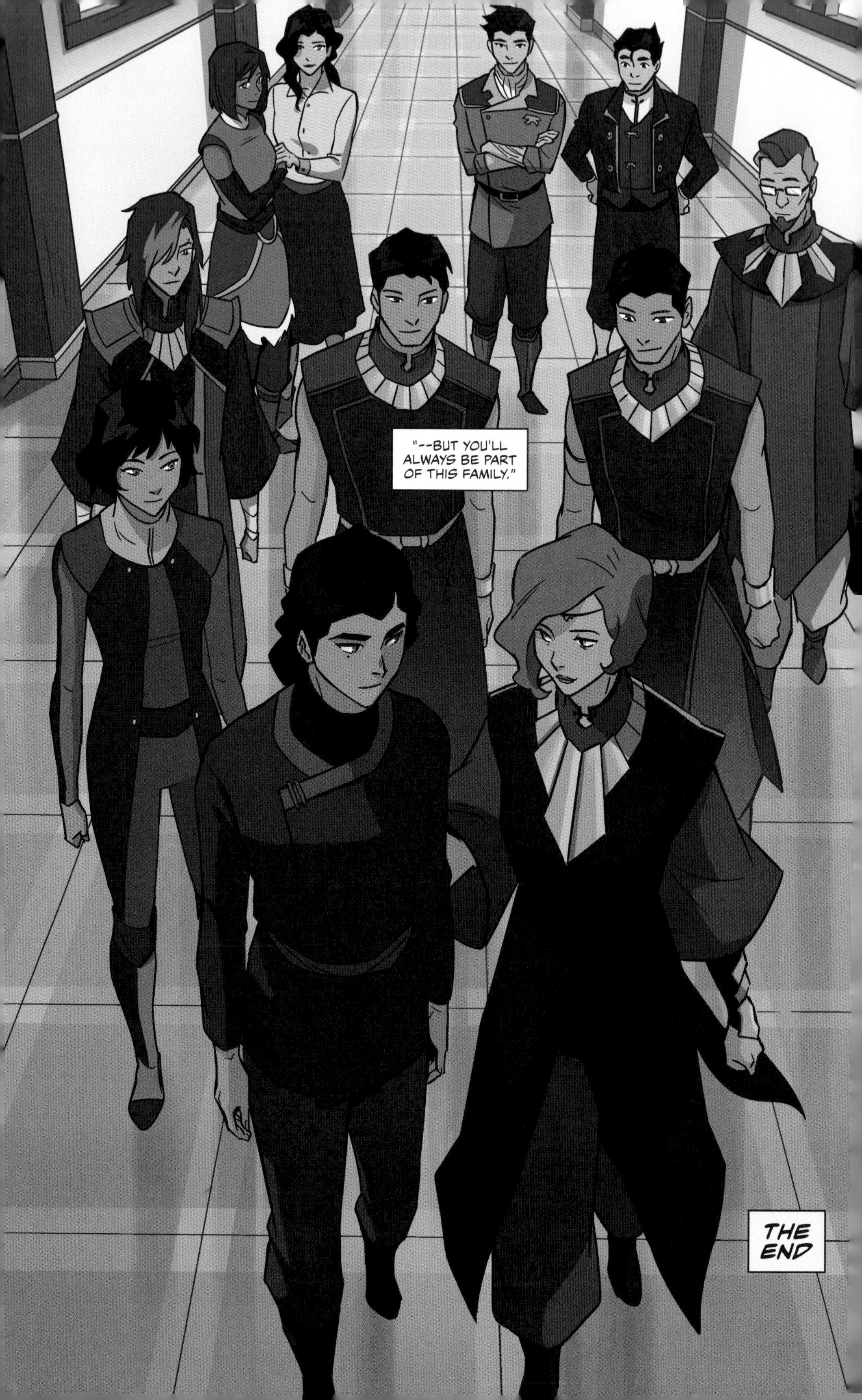
"--BUT YOU'LL ALWAYS BE PART OF THIS FAMILY."
THE END

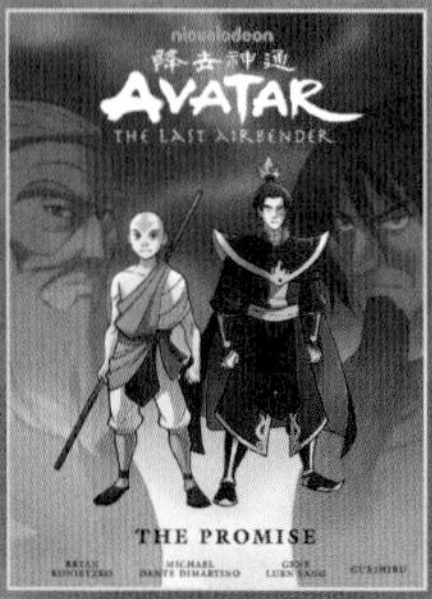
nickelodeon
AVATAR
THE LAST AIRBENDER
THE PROMISE

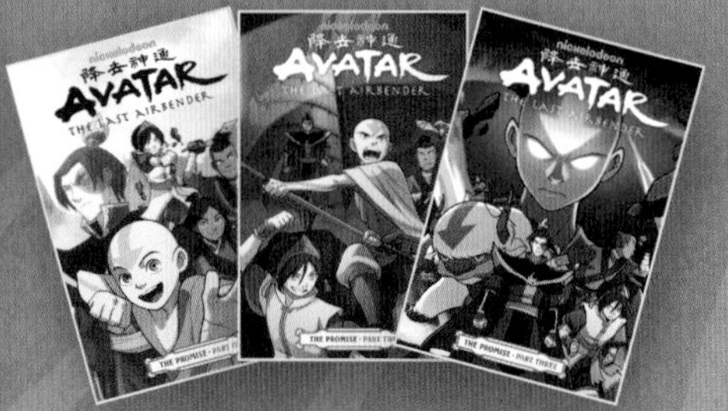

Avatar: The Last Airbender—The Promise Library Edition
978-1-61655-074-5 $39.99

Avatar: The Last Airbender—The Promise Part 1
978-1-59582-811-8 $10.99

Avatar: The Last Airbender—The Promise Part 2
978-1-59582-875-0 $10.99

Avatar: The Last Airbender—The Promise Part 3
978-1-59582-941-2 $10.99

Avatar: The Last Airbender—The Search Library Edition
978-1-61655-226-8 $39.99

Avatar: The Last Airbender—The Search Part 1
978-1-61655-054-7 $10.99

Avatar: The Last Airbender—The Search Part 2
978-1-61655-190-2 $10.99

Avatar: The Last Airbender—The Search Part 3
978-1-61655-184-1 $10.99

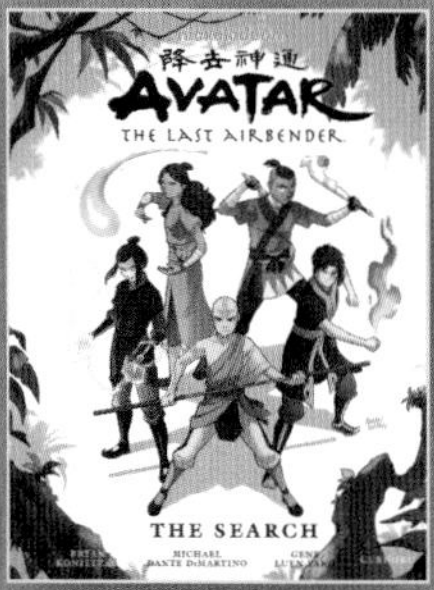
AVATAR
THE LAST AIRBENDER
THE SEARCH

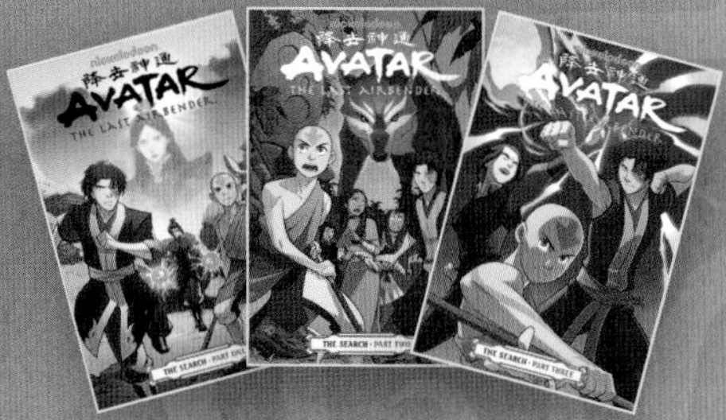

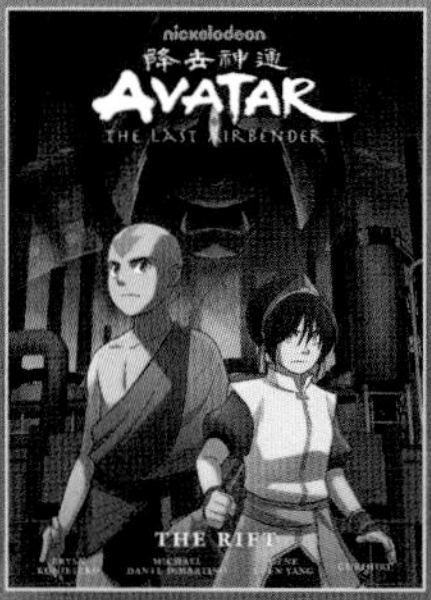
nickelodeon
AVATAR
THE LAST AIRBENDER
THE RIFT

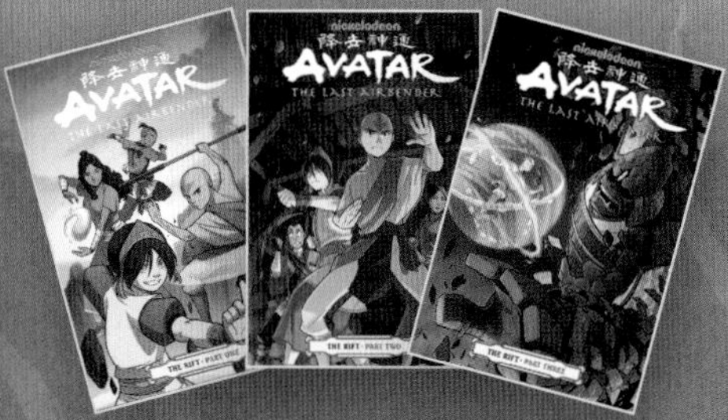

Avatar: The Last Airbender—The Rift Library Edition
978-1-61655-550-4 $39.99

Avatar: The Last Airbender—The Rift Part 1
978-1-61655-295-4 $10.99

Avatar: The Last Airbender—The Rift Part 2
978-1-61655-296-1 $10.99

Avatar: The Last Airbender—The Rift Part 3
978-1-61655-297-8 $10.99

Avatar: The Last Airbender—Smoke and Shadow Library Edition
978-1-50670-013-7 $39.99

Avatar: The Last Airbender—Smoke and Shadow Part 1
978-1-61655-761-4 $10.99

Avatar: The Last Airbender—Smoke and Shadow Part 2
978-1-61655-790-4 $10.99

Avatar: The Last Airbender—Smoke and Shadow Part 3
978-1-61655-838-3 $10.99

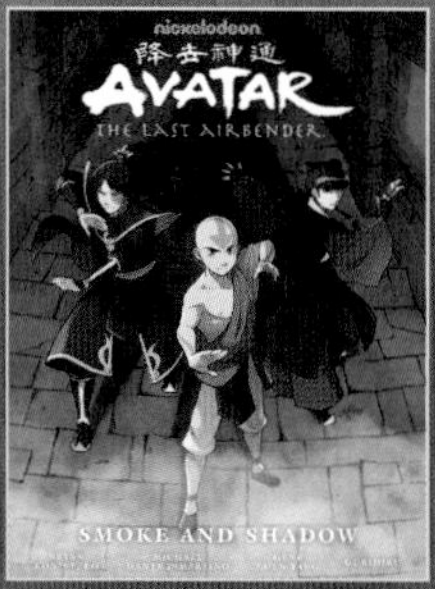
nickelodeon
AVATAR
THE LAST AIRBENDER
SMOKE AND SHADOW

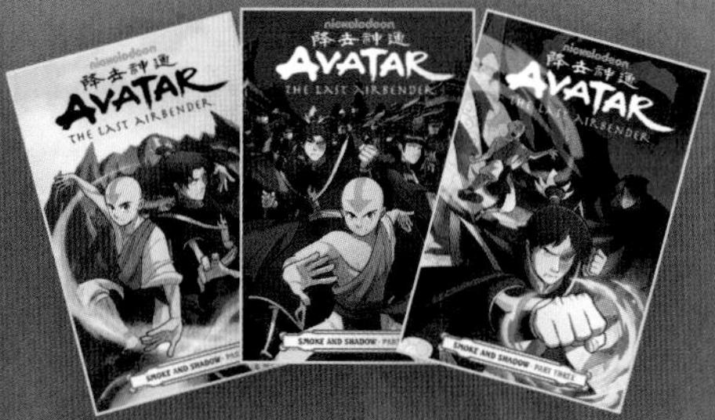

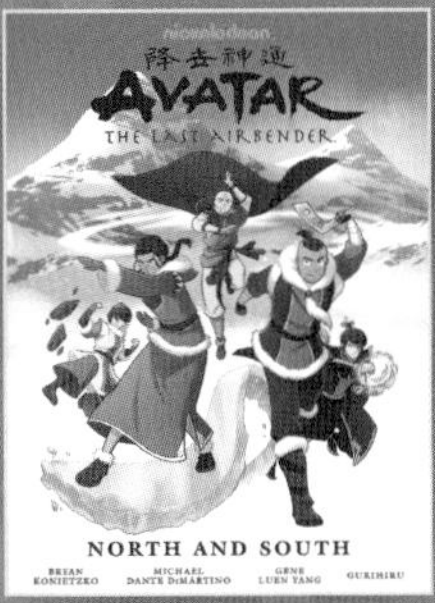
nickelodeon
降去神通
AVATAR
THE LAST AIRBENDER
NORTH AND SOUTH

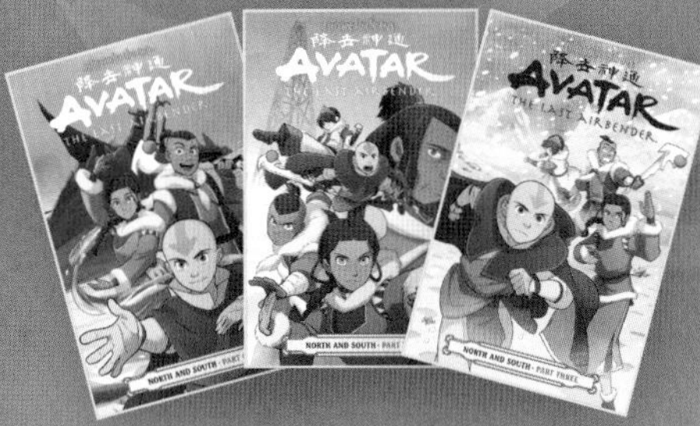

Avatar: The Last Airbender—North And South Library Edition
978-1-50670-195-0 $39.99

Avatar: The Last Airbender—North and South Part 1
978-1-50670-022-9 $10.99

Avatar: The Last Airbender—North and South Part 2
978-1-50670-129-5 $10.99

Avatar: The Last Airbender—North and South Part 3
978-1-50670-130-1 $10.99

nickelodeon

降去神通

AVATAR

THE LAST AIRBENDER

BE PART OF THE INCREDIBLE JOURNEY!

Check out the best-selling graphic novels and recapture the magic!

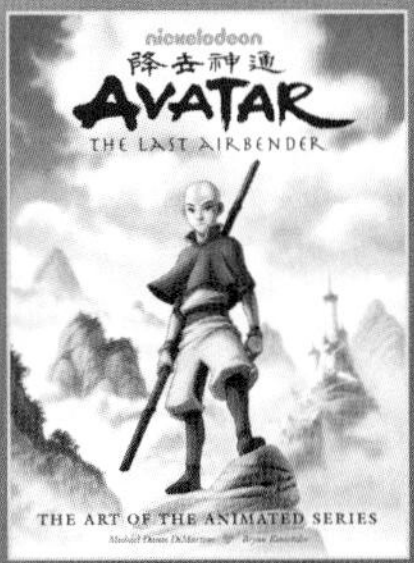
nickelodeon
降去神通
AVATAR
THE LAST AIRBENDER
THE ART OF THE ANIMATED SERIES

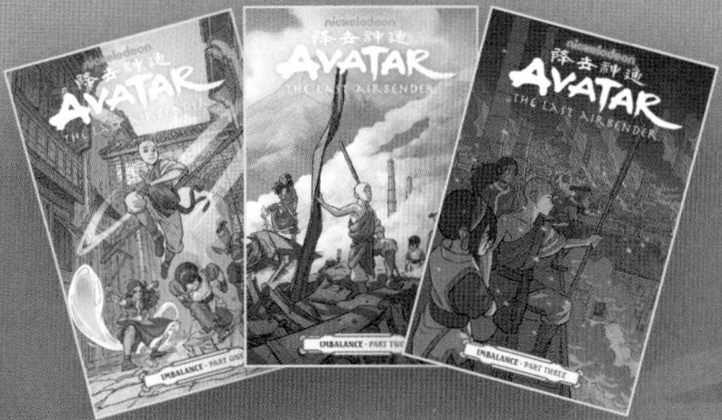

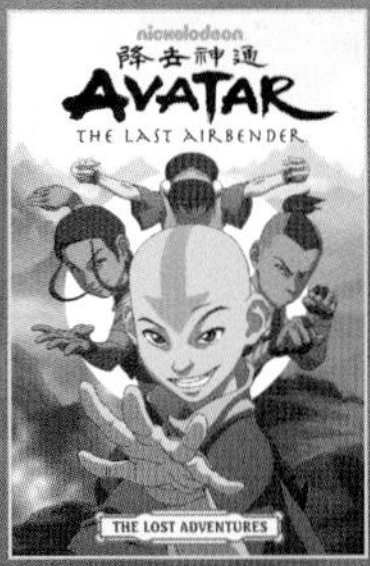
nickelodeon
降去神通
AVATAR
THE LAST AIRBENDER
THE LOST ADVENTURES

Avatar: The Last Airbender—Imbalance Part 1
978-1-50670-489-0 $10.99

Avatar: The Last Airbender—The Art of the Animated Series
978-1-59582-504-9 $34.99

Avatar: The Last Airbender—Imbalance Part 2
978-1-50670-652-8 $10.99

Avatar: The Last Airbender—Imbalance Part 3
978-1-50670-813-3 $10.99

Avatar: The Last Airbender—The Lost Adventures
978-1-59582-748-7 $14.99

AVAILABLE AT YOUR LOCAL COMICS SHOP OR BOOKSTORE! To find a comics shop in your area, visit comicshoplocator.com. For more information or to order direct visit DarkHorse.com or call 1-800-862-0052

DARK HORSE BOOKS

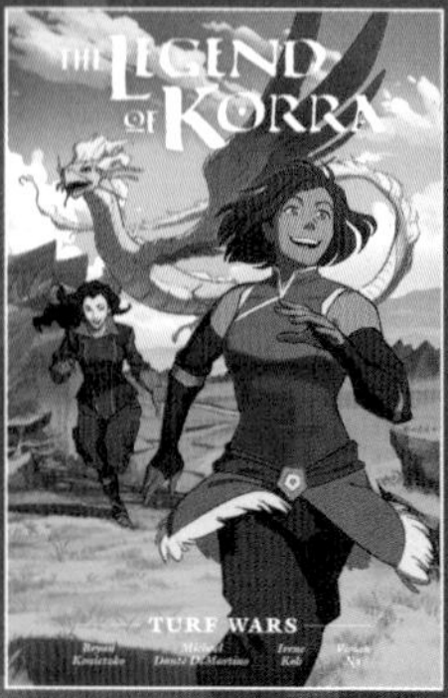
THE LEGEND OF KORRA
TURF WARS

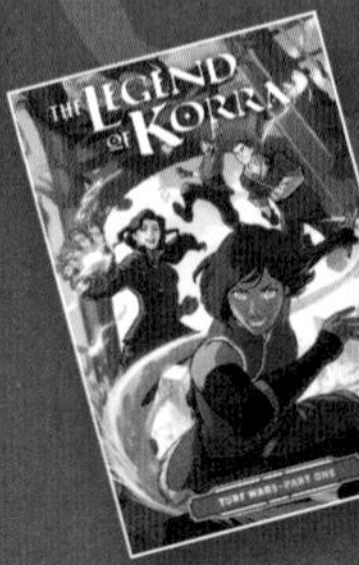
THE LEGEND OF KORRA
TURF WARS • PART ONE

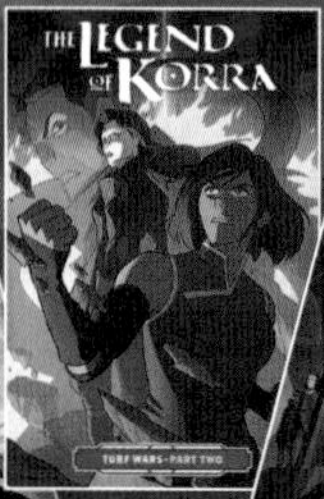
THE LEGEND OF KORRA
TURF WARS • PART TWO

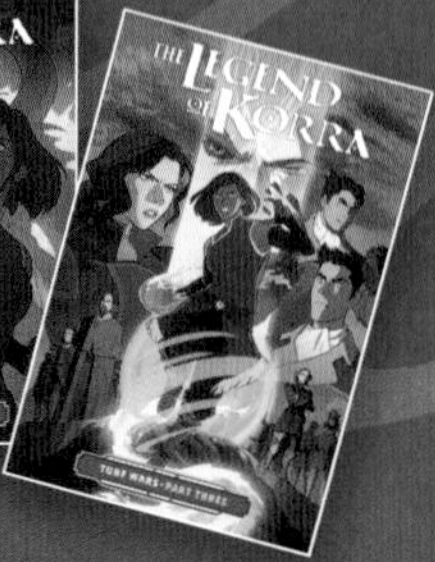
THE LEGEND OF KORRA
TURF WARS • PART THREE

The Legend of Korra: Turf Wars Library Editio
978-1-50670-202-5 $39.99

The Legend of Korra: Turf Wars Part One
978-1-50670-014-1 $10.99

The Legend of Korra: Turf Wars Part Two
978-1-50670-040-3 $10.99

The Legend of Korra: Turf Wars Part Three
978-1-50670-185-1 $10.99

nickelodeon

THE LEGEND OF KORRA

JOIN AVATAR KORRA AND TEAM AVATAR IN A NEW AGE OF ADVENTURE!

The Legend of Korra: The Animated Series Book One: Air
978-1-61655-168-1 $34.99

Book Two: Spirits
978-1-61655-462-0 $34.99

Book Three: Change
978-1-61655-565-8 $34.99

Book Four: Balance
978-1-61655-687-7 $34.99

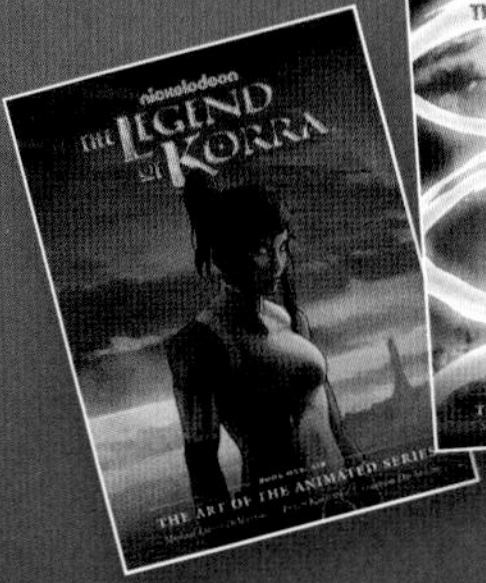
nickelodeon
THE LEGEND OF KORRA
THE ART OF THE ANIMATED SERIES

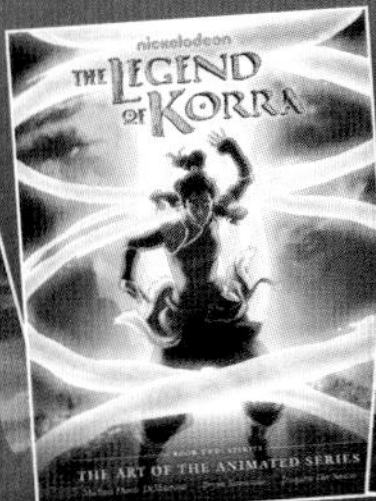
nickelodeon
THE LEGEND OF KORRA
THE ART OF THE ANIMATED SERIES

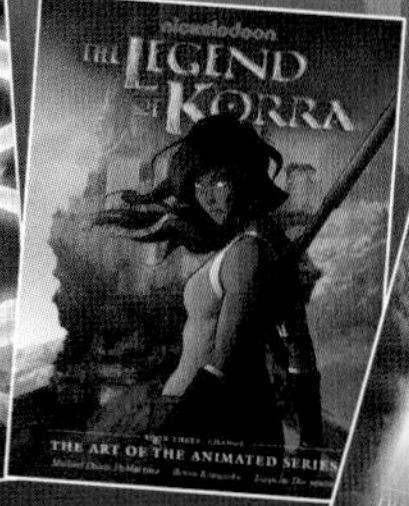
nickelodeon
THE LEGEND OF KORRA
THE ART OF THE ANIMATED SERIES

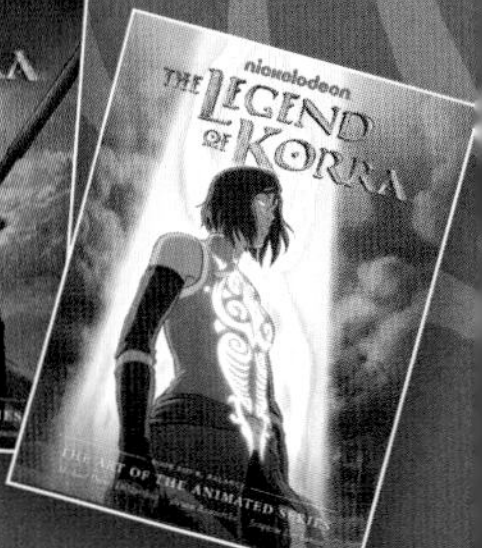
nickelodeon
THE LEGEND OF KORRA
THE ART OF THE ANIMATED SERIES

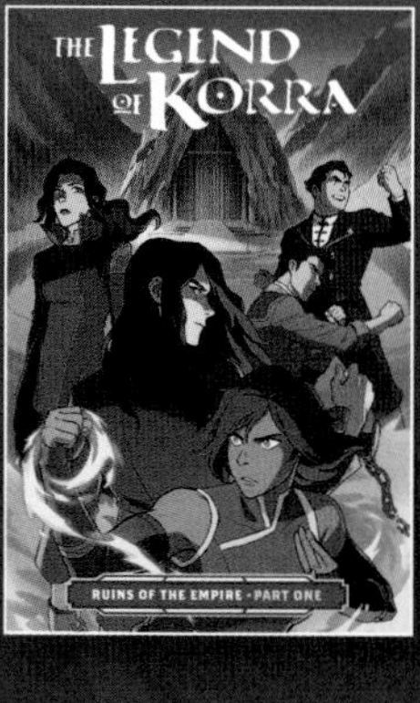
THE LEGEND OF KORRA
RUINS OF THE EMPIRE • PART ONE

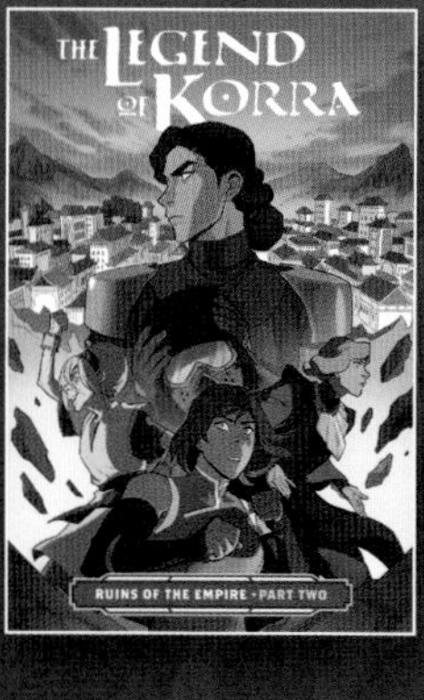
THE LEGEND OF KORRA
RUINS OF THE EMPIRE • PART TWO

The Legend of Korra: Ruins of the Empire Part One
978-1-50670-894-2 $10.99

The Legend of Korra: Ruins of the Empire Part Two
978-1-50670-895-9 $10.99

AVAILABLE AT YOUR LOCAL COMICS SHOP OR BOOKSTORE! To find a comics shop in your area, visit comicshoplocator.com. For more information or to order direct visit DarkHorse.com or email: mailorder@darkhorse.com

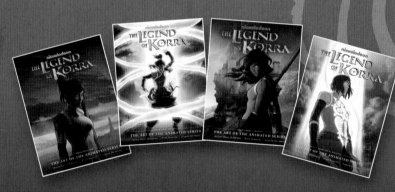